STEP INTO THE...
CELTIC WORLD

Fiona Macdonald

Consultant: Lloyd Laing, Nottingham University

LORENZ BOOKS

First published in 1999 by Lorenz Books
© Anness Publishing Limited 1999

Lorenz Books is an imprint of Anness Publishing
Limited, Hermes House, 88-89 Blackfriars Road,
London SE1 8HA

This edition published in the USA by Lorenz Books,
Anness Publishing Inc., 27 West 20th Street, New
York, NY 10011; (800) 354-9657

This edition distributed in Canada by Raincoast Books,
8680 Cambie Street, Vancouver, British Columbia,
V6P 6M9

ISBN 0 7548 0215 9
A CIP catalogue record for this book is available from
the British Library

Publisher: Joanna Lorenz
Managing Editor, Children's Books:
Gilly Cameron-Cooper
Senior Editor: Nicole Pearson
Editor: Nicola Barber
Designer: Caroline Reeves
Illustration: Rob Ashby, Vanessa Card, Shane Marsh
Special Photography: John Freeman
Stylist: Thomasina Smith

Anness Publishing would like to thank the following
children for modelling for this book: Anthony
Bainbridge, Sarah Bone, Louise Gannon, Bobbi
Graham, Karrine Gray, Daniel Haston, Isha Janneh,
Liliana Conceicao de Jesus, Eka Karumidze,
Muhammed Laher, Bianca S. Loucaides, Gabriel Nipah,
Daniel A. Otalvora, Sarah Phillips, Charlie Emilin Ray,
Tom Swaine-Jameson.

PICTURE CREDITS
b=bottom, t=top, c=centre, l=left, r=right
AKG London: 4tl, 10tl, 11c, 12tr, 16tl, 17c, 17tl, 18tl, 18bl,
19br, 19tr, 20br, 21tr, 22tl, 34bl, 42tl, 44tl, 47tr, 48tl, 49bl,
49br, 54tl, 55c, 57bl, 58tl, 58bl, 59tl, 61tr; Ancient Art &
Architecture Collection: 13tl, 56br, 61tl; Sheridan/AAA
Collection: 8tr, 17tr, 25tr, 44c, 54c; Charles Tait/AAA
Collection 51bl; Musée des antiquités: 4tr; Bridgeman Art
Library, London: Mount with champleve decoration 11tl,
"Etain, Helen, Maeve, and Fand, Golden Deirdre's Tender
Hand" by Harry Clarke 43bl; C M Dixon: 10b, 11br, 12br,
14tl, 16br, 20tl, 23tl, 23tr, 32tl, 33bl, 35tl, 36tl, 36c, 37tr,
37c, 38br, 39tl, 39bl, 40tl, 41tl, 41c, 42c, 43tr, 43br, 45tr,
45bl, 45c, 46tl, 48c, 49tl, 55tl, 55tl, 59br; Peter
Dobson/Celtica: 19tl; E.T. Archive: 9tl, 13tr, 13bl, 21c; Fine
Art Photographic Library: 24c; T.E. Grey: 52; Michael Holford:
13br; Jenny Laing: 25tl, 25bl, 27c, 47bl; Musée Calvet, Avignon:
14br; Musée Archaeologique, Chatillon-sur-Seine: 8tl; National
Museum of Wales: 15br Stuart Rae: 51tr; Roman Baths
Museum: 55bl; Scotland in Focus: 9tr, 29tl, 35tl, 51tl, 60tl;
Mick Sharp: 24tl, 27tl, 28tl, 29bl, 29br, 31tr, 50tl, 57tl, 61c;
Skyscan: 21tl, 25br, 26bl, 28bl, 35br, Charles Tait/Mick Sharp:
27tr; The Trustees of the National Museums of Scotland 1999:
37bl, 43tl; Keith Welch: 37tl; Werner Forman: 5c, 5tl, 9c,
11bl, 15bl, 19bl, 20bl, 21bl, 23bl, 23c, 26tl, 30tl, 32bl, 32br,
34br, 34tl, 40c, 41bl, 46bl, 47bl, 50bl, 56tl, 59bl.

Printed and bound in Singapore
10 9 8 7 6 5 4 3 2 1

CONTENTS

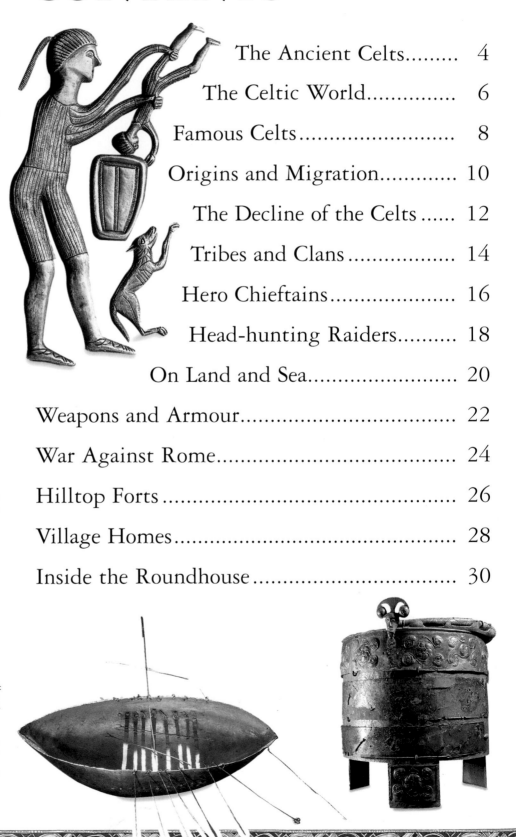

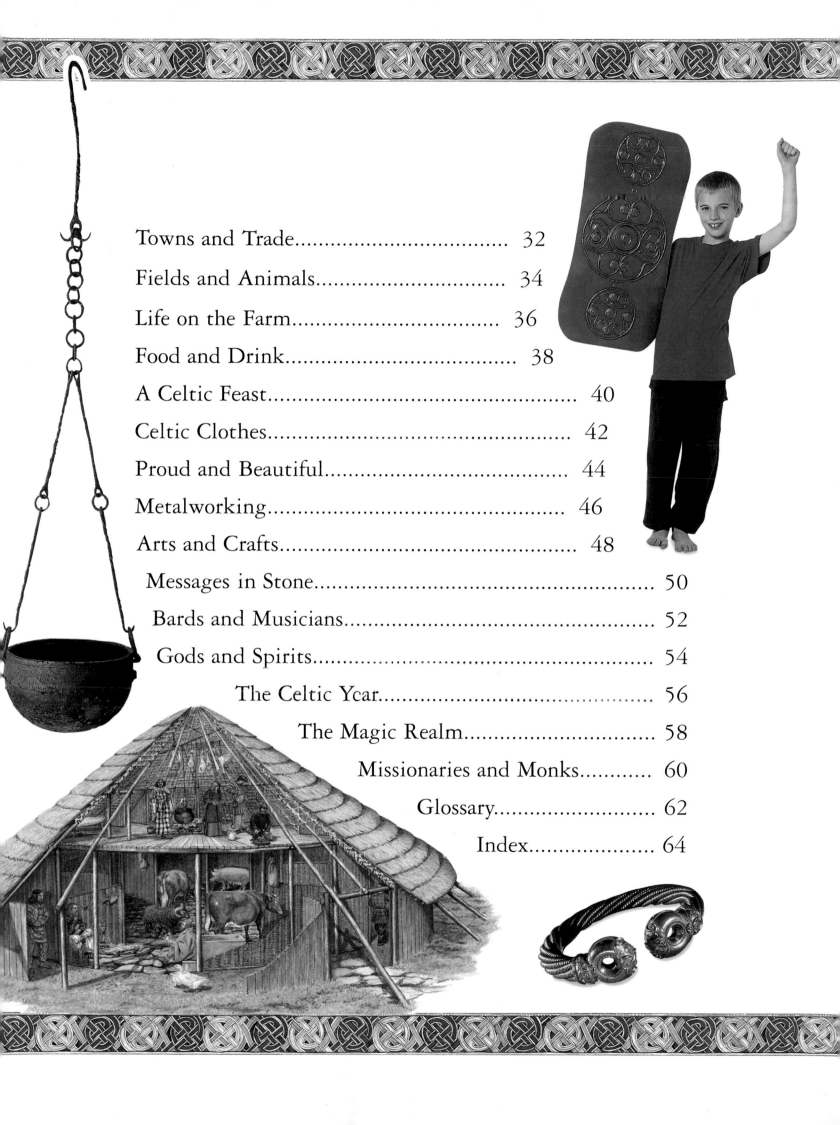

The Ancient Celts

FROM AROUND 750BC TO 12BC, the Celts were the most powerful people in central and northern Europe. There were many groups (sometimes called tribes) of Celts. They spoke related languages, shared similar, but not identical, technologies, customs and beliefs, and created works of art in closely connected styles. Their civilization flourished across a vast area, from the British Isles to the borders of Ukraine. However, there was never one single Celtic nation, language or lifestyle. Celtic traditions developed at different times and in different places. The Celts also borrowed many ideas and designs from other European peoples, including the Greeks, the Etruscans and Romans (from Italy), and the Scythians (from the Black Sea area).

WAR-MAD?
This bronze statue of a Celtic warrior god has fierce, staring eyes of shiny glass paste. It was made in France during the 1st century BC. Around the time the statue was created, the Greek geographer Strabo described the Celts as "war-mad ... high-spirited and quick for battle".

MYSTERIOUS GOD
An unknown Celtic god is portrayed in this stone statue from France. Similar statues made from stone or wood stood in the Celts' most holy shrines. The god has a wild boar on his chest, and round his neck he wears a torc (heavy necklace). The Celts believed that torcs had magic power.

TIMELINE c.800–400BC

Celtic civilization flourished from about 750BC to 12BC, but some Celtic ideas, beliefs and traditions continued in north-west Europe for another 700 years.

c.800–600BC Groups of horsemen with long iron swords and wheeled chariots become powerful in central Europe.

c.800–600BC New defences are built

example of early Celtic metalwork

around many European villages, probably to defend them from Celtic attack. At the same time, long-distance trade is disrupted, and production of fine craftwork slows down.

c.750–500BC The new technology of ironworking becomes popular in central Europe.

rucksack from the salt mines in Hallstatt

c.700–450BC The miners, merchants, craftworkers and soldiers living in and around the salt mines at Hallstatt, Austria, become rich and powerful. Their salt is traded throughout central Europe. It is highly prized for preserving food and as medicine for cattle.

c.700 450BC The Hallstatt people are ruled by Celtic warrior families; they can afford new iron weapons, as well as fine bronze vessels and gold jewellery.

Celtic farmers

c.800BC   750BC   700BC   650BC   600BC

SIMPLE SCRIPT

The Celts had no written script of their own. For important monuments, such as this standing stone from Ireland, they borrowed scripts used by neighbouring peoples. This inscription is carved in Ogham – a script based on the Roman alphabet, but using lines instead of letters. It is difficult to discover everything we would like to know about the Celts because they did not keep detailed written records.

METALWORK

The Celts were famous throughout Europe for their skill as metalworkers. This bronze disc was made to decorate a horse harness in about 450BC. It was found by archaeologists in a Celtic burial site in France. Archaeologists have been investigating the remains of Celtic civilization, such as burial sites, for over 200 years. During that time, they have made many remarkable discoveries, including rich tombs and beautiful jewellery.

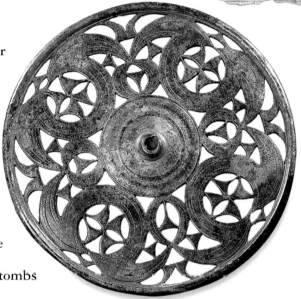

KEY

Hallstatt culture (750–450BC)

La Tène culture (450–50BC)

THE CELTIC HEARTLANDS

This map shows the parts of Europe where archaeologists have found some of the best-preserved evidence for Celtic culture. The Hallstatt region of Austria was the richest, most powerful part of the Celtic lands from around 750 to 450BC. Later, from around 450 to 50BC, the La Tène region of Switzerland became one of the leading centres of the Celtic civilization.

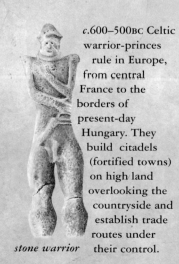

*c.*600–500BC Celtic warrior-princes rule in Europe, from central France to the borders of present-day Hungary. They build citadels (fortified towns) on high land overlooking the countryside and establish trade routes under their control.

stone warrior

*c.*520BC A 35-year-old woman is buried in a wood-lined chamber at Vix in eastern France. Alongside her are personal ornaments, a dismantled burial wagon and imported drinking vessels. The woman wears a massive torc around her neck containing almost half a kilo of pure gold.

Vix krater (wine serving bowl)

*c.*500BC Celtic society becomes more equal. Warrior princes abandon their citadels and live closer to farmers, traders and craftworkers. Celtic culture reaches Brittany and possibly as far as parts of northern Spain.

*c.*450BC La Tène style of art develops in central Europe producing some of the finest Celtic art objects.

La Tène statue

550BC   500BC   450BC   400BC

The Celtic World

Atlantic Ocean

Oppidum (fortifi[ed]
town) of Citania
de Sanfins

Iberian
fortified settlem[ent]

THE STORY OF THE CELTS begins between 750BC and 600BC. At this time, Celtic warrior chieftains began to ride on horseback and to arm themselves with long swords. When they died, they were buried in magnificent tombs containing wagons with iron-rimmed wheels and sumptuous gold jewellery. These extravagant burials tell us that the Celtic peoples were both powerful and wealthy. The Celts' power came from their strength as horse-riding warriors. They became wealthy from the profitable salt and copper mines around Hallstatt in Austria, and from the trade in valuable goods and raw materials (such as iron ore) with peoples who lived further south. By around 550BC, the Celts were building citadels (fortified towns) to dominate the surrounding land.

The years from 400BC to 200BC were a time of migrations. Celts moved northwards to Germany and southwards to Italy. In 350BC, they invaded western Hungary, then headed south into Greece. In 279BC they attacked the Greeks' holiest shrine, the temple of Apollo at Delphi, but were driven away. Another group of Celts settled in Turkey around 240BC. At the same time, Celtic peoples moved into south-western France, Spain and Portugal. This brought them face to face with the Roman army – the strongest fighting force in Europe. For the next 200 years, Romans and Celts were at war. By around AD60, Celtic power was almost completely destroyed. Only in remote areas such as Brittany, Scotland, Ireland and Wales did Celtic traditions survive.

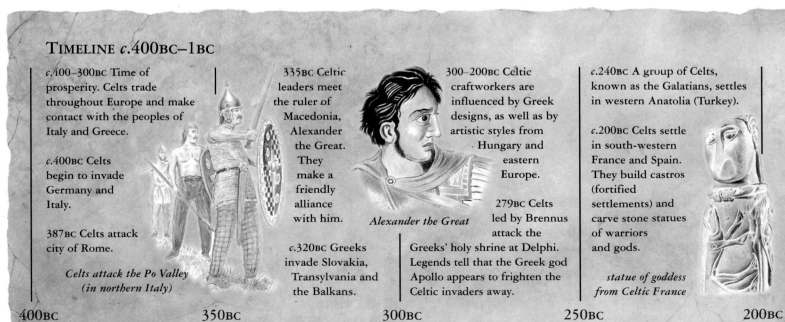

TIMELINE c.400BC–1BC

c.400–300BC Time of prosperity. Celts trade throughout Europe and make contact with the peoples of Italy and Greece.

c.400BC Celts begin to invade Germany and Italy.

387BC Celts attack city of Rome.

Celts attack the Po Valley (in northern Italy)

335BC Celtic leaders meet the ruler of Macedonia, Alexander the Great. They make a friendly alliance with him.

c.320BC Greeks invade Slovakia, Transylvania and the Balkans.

Alexander the Great

300–200BC Celtic craftworkers are influenced by Greek designs, as well as by artistic styles from Hungary and eastern Europe.

279BC Celts led by Brennus attack the Greeks' holy shrine at Delphi. Legends tell that the Greek god Apollo appears to frighten the Celtic invaders away.

c.240BC A group of Celts, known as the Galatians, settles in western Anatolia (Turkey).

c.200BC Celts settle in south-western France and Spain. They build castros (fortified settlements) and carve stone statues of warriors and gods.

statue of goddess from Celtic France

400BC	350BC	300BC	250BC	200BC

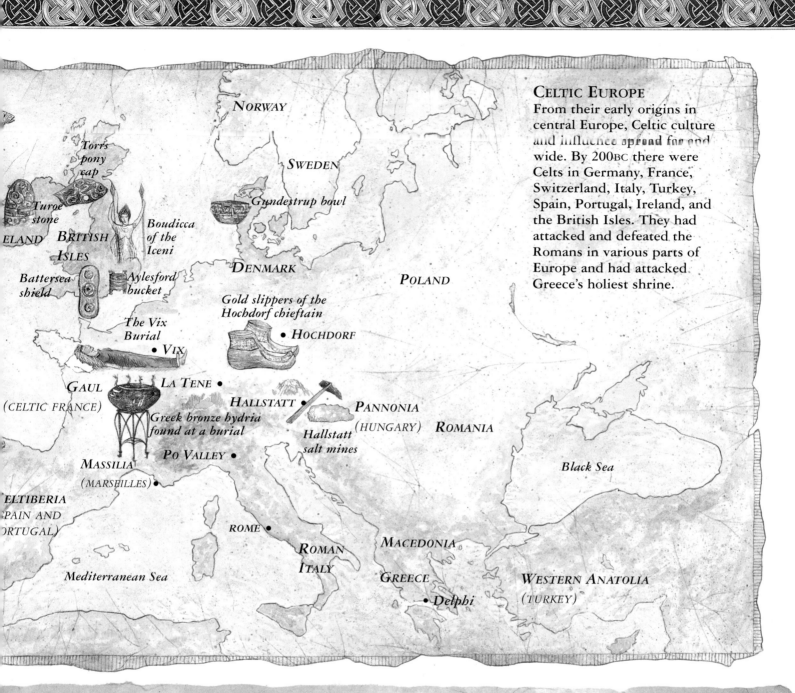

CELTIC EUROPE

From their early origins in central Europe, Celtic culture and influence spread far and wide. By 200BC there were Celts in Germany, France, Switzerland, Italy, Turkey, Spain, Portugal, Ireland, and the British Isles. They had attacked and defeated the Romans in various parts of Europe and had attacked Greece's holiest shrine.

NORWAY

SWEDEN

Torrs pony cap

Turoe stone

ELAND

BRITISH ISLES

Boudicca of the Iceni

Gundestrup bowl

Battersea shield

Aylesford bucket

DENMARK

POLAND

Gold slippers of the Hochdorf chieftain

HOCHDORF

The Vix Burial

VIX

GAUL
(CELTIC FRANCE)

LA TENE

Greek bronze hydria found at a burial

HALLSTATT

Hallstatt salt mines

PANNONIA
(HUNGARY)

ROMANIA

PO VALLEY

MASSILIA
(MARSEILLES)

Black Sea

ELTIBERIA
(PAIN AND
ORTUGAL)

ROME

ROMAN ITALY

MACEDONIA

GREECE

Delphi

WESTERN ANATOLIA
(TURKEY)

Mediterranean Sea

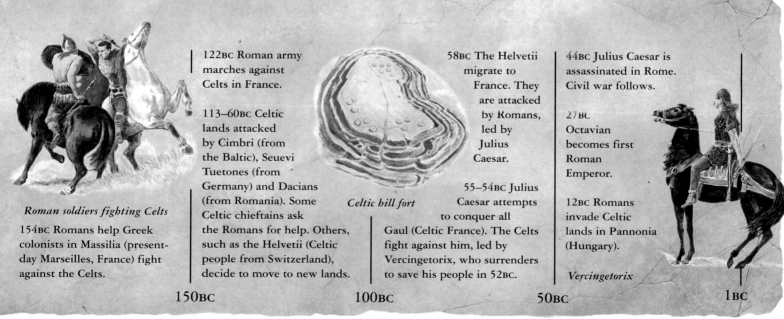

Roman soldiers fighting Celts

122BC Roman army marches against Celts in France.

113–60BC Celtic lands attacked by Cimbri (from the Baltic), Seuevi Tuetones (from Germany) and Dacians (from Romania). Some Celtic chieftains ask the Romans for help. Others, such as the Helvetii (Celtic people from Switzerland), decide to move to new lands.

Celtic hill fort

154BC Romans help Greek colonists in Massilia (present-day Marseilles, France) fight against the Celts.

58BC The Helvetii migrate to France. They are attacked by Romans, led by Julius Caesar.

55–54BC Julius Caesar attempts to conquer all Gaul (Celtic France). The Celts fight against him, led by Vercingetorix, who surrenders to save his people in 52BC.

44BC Julius Caesar is assassinated in Rome. Civil war follows.

27BC Octavian becomes first Roman Emperor.

12BC Romans invade Celtic lands in Pannonia (Hungary).

Vercingetorix

150BC   100BC   50BC   1BC

Famous Celts

Even though the Celts did not keep written records, we know the names of some people who lived in Celtic times. This is because people who could read and write, such as Greek geographers and Roman army commanders, described some of the Celtic leaders they came across. To the Celts themselves, being respected was more important than life itself. The legendary Irish hero, Cuchulainn, was reported to have said: "So long as I am famous, I do not care if I live for just one day in this world." The qualities that the Celts most admired were bravery, wealth and generosity. Rulers who owned rich treasures and wore magnificent jewels were admired for bringing honour to their tribe by their glittering display of wealth. Fierce war-leaders such as Boudicca, Cunobelinus and Vercingetorix were praised for their courage and bravery when faced with death. Even after Celtic power faded away, adventurous missionaries such as St Columba worked to win fame for the Christian faith.

BURIED TREASURE
This Celtic princess was buried at Vix, in eastern France, around 520BC. Her tomb is one of the most splendid ever discovered in Europe, and contained rich treasures from as far away as Greece. The princess was wearing a torc made of almost half a kilogram of pure gold.

HERO OF FRANCE
Vercingetorix led the Gauls (the Celtic people of France) in their last fight against the Romans in 52BC. He bravely surrendered in order to allow his followers to escape death.

TIMELINE AD1–1066

AD1 End of Celtic power in mainland Europe. Celtic traditions continue in isolated regions, such as Brittany.

Boudicca

AD43 Romans conquer southern Britain.

AD60 Queen Boudicca of the Celtic Iceni tribe (from eastern England) leads a rebellion against the Romans.

AD61 Boudicca is defeated. End of Celtic power in England.

AD122 Roman emperor, Hadrian, builds a wall across northern England to defend Roman lands from Celts to the north. Celtic culture mingles with, and is largely absorbed by, Roman

Hadrian's Wall

culture in southern Britain. Celtic influence continues, in part, in Scotland, Wales and Ireland. Descendants of Celtic chiefs continue to rule in these three areas.

AD410 Romans withdraw from Britain.

AD432 Christian missionary, St Patrick, brings the Christian faith to Ireland. From now on, Irish monks copy Celtic traditions, especially in art. They also help to preserve ancient Celtic stories and beliefs by writing them down in manuscripts.

a Christian saint

AD1

AD250

AD500

BRITISH KING

This beautiful gold coin was made for Cunobelinus, one of the last Celtic chieftains. He ruled lands in south-east England from around AD10 to AD40. His sons led the Celtic fight against the Roman conquerors of Britain.

CELTIC SAINT

St Columba was born into a Celtic family in Ireland in AD521. He became a Christian monk and spent many years preaching in Ireland. In AD563 he went to Scotland where he founded a monastery on the island of Iona. From there, he and his monks took news of the Christian faith to the peoples of Scotland.

WARRIOR QUEEN

Boudicca was wife of the ruler of the Iceni, a Celtic people who lived in eastern England. After her husband's death, the Romans claimed the Iceni lands. When Boudicca protested she was beaten and her daughters raped. In revenge, Boudicca led an army to attack London in AD60–1. Boudicca's army caused vast amounts of damage before being defeated.

AD500 onwards Britain is invaded by Angles and Saxons. They introduce a new Germanic language and culture.

c.AD560 Irish monks re-introduce Celtic artistic traditions to England, along with their Christian religious teachings. They decorate Christian texts and monuments with swirling Celtic designs.

AD563–597 The Christian missionary, St Columba, sets up a monastery on the island of Iona, off the west coast of Scotland. It becomes a centre of Christian, Celtic art and learning.

the Book of Durrow

AD675 *Book of Durrow* is written in the monastery at Durrow reputedly by St Columba himself.

c.AD790 First Viking raid on Britain. The Vikings introduce their own language and culture.

c.AD800 *Book of Kells* is produced in Ireland. It is one of the last masterpieces of late Celtic art. It contains the Christian Gospels as well as Irish texts.

a Celtic cross

1066 Normans (Vikings who had settled in France) invade Britain. Last traces of Celtic culture disappear in British Isles. But a few traces remain in folk songs, myths and legends, and in the Gaelic, Welsh, Cornish and Manx languages.

AD750

AD1000

Origins and Migration

Historians used to think that the Celts were a single ethnic group who originated in one place, north of the Black Sea, then spread across Europe. However, this view has since been challenged. Most experts now believe that the Celts were descended from earlier inhabitants of northern Europe. They also think that the Celts were not one ethnic group, but many different peoples who shared a similar way of life that changed and developed over the centuries between around 800BC and AD100.

There were some major movements (migrations) of Celtic tribes, mostly from Celtic lands to non-Celtic countries in Europe. In about 400BC, it seems that some parts of France became overcrowded. Celtic warriors, farmers and their families set out towards Germany and Italy. One group settled south of the Alps, on fertile land in northern Italy. In 350BC, more Celtic migrants moved into western Hungary, Slovakia and Transylvania. Soon afterwards, they headed southwards into Greece and Bulgaria. There is not much evidence to suggest that there were large-scale migrations from mainland Europe into the British Isles. It seems that local Celtic civilization developed independently in Britain.

There were also many links between British, Irish and European Celtic peoples through long-distance trade.

TYPICAL LA TÈNE
Historians divide the Celtic age into two main sections, the Hallstatt era (from about 750BC to 450BC) and the La Tène era (from about 450BC to 50BC). Both eras are named after types of Celtic art. Fine metalwork and rich burials are typical of the Hallstatt era. Elaborate, swirling designs, such as the ones on this carved stone pillar, are typical of the art of the La Tène era.

RICHES FROM SALT
This drawing of a Hallstatt burial was made in about 1860. Over 2,000 burials have been discovered at the Austrian town of Hallstatt, most dating from 800–600BC. Around 800BC, the Celts living near Hallstatt began to grow rich and powerful because they controlled the salt trade. They buried their dead with precious goods such as jewellery and daggers.

IRON AND SALT

The Celts discovered how to mine and process the iron ore and salt in their lands. They exchanged iron objects and salt for goods with merchants from all over Europe. Iron ore (left) and rock salt (right) were very valuable commodities. Iron was used to make sharp, long-lasting weapons and tools, and it also had prestige value. Salt was used in medicines and to preserve food.

iron ore   *rock salt*

ART FROM THE EAST

This bronze harness mount was made in Ukraine in about AD100. It shows that Celtic designs were popular on the eastern frontiers of Europe, and that Celtic metalworking skills were also known there. Like many pieces of Celtic art, it is decorated with patterns based on spiral shapes.

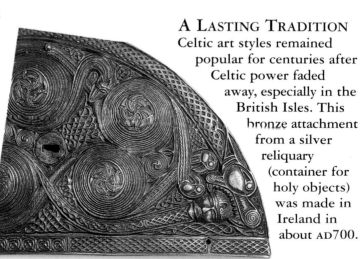

MOUNTED HUNTER

At the beginning of the Hallstatt era (750–450BC), big, strong horses were introduced into western Europe from the lands east of the Black Sea. These mounts gave Celtic hunters and warriors a great advantage. This bronze statue shows a Celtic hunter on horseback, mounted on a burial wagon.

A SHARED STYLE

Wherever they lived in Europe, Celtic craftworkers decorated the objects they made using similar styles and techniques. This pottery vessel was made in about 350BC. It is decorated with lines scratched into the clay. The pattern featured on the vessel is also found on metalwork created during the period.

A LASTING TRADITION

Celtic art styles remained popular for centuries after Celtic power faded away, especially in the British Isles. This bronze attachment from a silver reliquary (container for holy objects) was made in Ireland in about AD700.

The Decline of the Celts

CELTIC POWER in Europe lasted for around 800 years. As it declined, Celtic lands were divided among many other peoples who had grown strong enough to make their own claims for power. The first people to fight against the Celts were also the most formidable – the well-trained, well-equipped soldiers of the Roman empire. The Romans managed to drive the Celtic settlers out of northern Italy in 191BC. They took control of Spain in 133BC and, after long campaigns led by the brilliant general, Julius Caesar, finally conquered France in 51BC. Roman armies invaded southern Britain in AD43. At first there was resistance, such as the revolt led by the Celtic queen, Boudicca. Nevertheless, by AD61 the Romans controlled southern Britain, and they ruled there until AD410. However, the Romans never managed to conquer all the British Isles. Parts of Scotland and Ireland continued under Celtic rule until about AD1100. As Roman power weakened, new groups of migrants arrived, mostly from the north, to settle in the former Celtic lands. These invaders included many peoples with strong armies and vibrant cultures of their own, such as the Visigoths, the Angles and Saxons, the Franks, and the Vikings.

GREAT CONQUEROR

Julius Caesar (*c.*100–44BC) led the Roman armies that conquered the Celts in France. He fought and won a series of battles, known as the Gallic Wars, between 58BC and 51BC. He also hoped to conquer Britain and Germany, but a political crisis in Italy forced him to return to Rome.

ROMAN STYLE

After the Romans conquered Britain in AD43, a new, mixed civilization grew up which combined both Roman and Celtic traditions. Although some Celtic chieftains rebelled against Roman rule, others decided to co-operate with the Romans, and served as local governors. They built splendid country houses, known as villas, which were decorated in the Roman style with beautiful mosaic floors such as this one.

THE VISIGOTHS

This jewelled, golden crown was made for the Visigothic kings of Spain to give as a religious offering. The Visigoths were a people from northern Europe. Celtic lands in Spain were conquered by the Romans in 133BC, and then by the Visigoths in about AD400. Even so, many Celtic skills, such as the art of fine metalworking, survived and were passed down by successive generations of settlers.

KING OF THE FRANKS

The Romans ruled France until about AD400. Northern France was then taken over by the Franks, a people from southern Germany. The Frankish kings built up a powerful empire in former Celtic France. Their most successful and powerful ruler was King Charlemagne (left), who reigned from AD771 to 814.

SAXON KING

This fine, metal helmet was made for an Anglo-Saxon warrior king. The king was buried at Sutton Hoo, on the east coast of England, the land that Boudicca once ruled. The Angles and Saxons came from southern Denmark and north-western Germany. They settled in southern England, where they established seven separate kingdoms.

VIKING WARRIORS

The Vikings were sailors, raiders and traders who came from Scandinavia. They first attacked Britain around AD790. Soon afterwards, Viking settlers came to live in many parts of the British Isles and northern France. This tombstone shows two Viking warriors with round shields.

Tribes and Clans

THE CELTS WERE NEVER a single, unified nation. Instead there were many separate Celtic tribes throughout Europe. Greek and Roman writers recorded many Celtic tribal names, for example, the Helvetii (who lived in Switzerland) and the Caledones (who lived in Scotland). Tribes sometimes made friendly alliances with one another, or with a stronger power such as Rome. This usually happened when a tribe was threatened by invaders or at war. Within each tribe, there were many clans. These were families who traced their descent from a single ancestor, and who shared ties of loyalty and a family name.

Each tribe was headed by a king (or chieftain). His task was to lead men in battle and on raids, and to maintain peace and prosperity. Kings were chosen from rich noble families. Senior noblemen were expected to support the king and to lead their own bands of warriors. Druids (Celtic priests) and bards (well-educated poets) also came from noble families. Farmers and craftworkers ranked lower, but they were highly valued for their important skills. There were also servants and slaves.

GUARDIAN GODDESS

Many Celtic tribes had their own special god or goddess, to protect them and to bring fertility to their farm animals and crops. This mother goddess was the special guardian of a Celtic tribe who lived in Austria. She is shown gently cradling twin babies on her lap – a vivid reminder of her magical protective powers. After a battle, the Celts sacrificed a share of all they had captured to their favourite gods and goddesses.

PROUD LEADER

This stone statue portrays a Celtic king or chieftain from Gaul (present-day France). It was made around 50BC. He is dressed ready to lead his tribe into war, in a chain mail tunic and a magic torc. His torc is an indication of high rank, but we have no idea who he actually was.

Religious support, knowledge, rituals

Protection and offerings

Chieftains

Gifts and prestige

Loyalty and help in battle

Druids and bards

Protection and offerings

Religious support

Farmers and craftworkers

Nobles and warriors

Religious support

Respect and offerings

Respect and manpower

Protection and access to land

THE STRUCTURE OF SOCIETY

All the different groups within Celtic society had an important part to play, and they all relied on one another to survive. This diagram shows what each different group gave to society, and what it received in return. Chieftains offered leadership and inspired loyalty, while nobles and warriors protected the tribe from attack. Druids and bards provided religious support and celebrated tribal pride. Farmers and craftworkers produced food and goods. The lowest social rank was held by labourers and slaves. They did jobs that were often hard and dirty.

TRIBAL COIN

Many Celtic tribes issued coins, marked with their own special design. This coin was made for the Catuvellauni tribe who lived in southern England. It shows a warrior on horseback riding into battle brandishing a carnyx (war-trumpet). It was designed to tell everyone what a brave and warlike people the Catuvellauni were.

SLAVE CHAIN

Chains like these were used to stop slaves running away. The round iron bracelets, joined by links of heavy metal, were fastened round a slave's wrists or ankles and locked shut. Slavery was never very important in Celtic society. There were many more free people than slaves. However, slaves were used for dirty, difficult, dangerous work (for example, in the salt mines at Hallstatt).

Hero Chieftains

Strength, boldness, boastfulness, courage — these were the qualities that made a Celtic hero. Brave Celtic warriors often fought as individual champions, parading in front of the enemy before a battle, boasting of their brave deeds and those of their ancestors, and daring anyone to fight against them. Chieftains might also be accompanied to the battlefield by a parasite, the name for a low-ranking follower who had the task of praising the chieftain and his exploits in war. Sometimes, a war was settled by two hero chieftains fighting one another.

All Celtic warriors knew that a battle might well lead to death, but they did not show fear. This was partly because bands of warriors worked themselves up into a state of fury as they prepared for a fight, to give each other courage. They also drank large amounts of strong ale or wine. The din of drums and war-trumpets may have helped to induce a trance-like state. The Celts' beliefs helped them face death and danger, too. Celtic people thought that their spirits would not die, even though their bodies were killed. They believed that it was better to die in battle than to survive and face defeat. Defeat led to deep disgrace, and often suicide.

ELITE WARRIOR
A Celtic warrior hero from Germany is portrayed in this sandstone statue from around 550BC. The warrior wears a torc and a sword-belt. His conical helmet would have been made of metal. Similar helmets have been found in the graves of many Celtic warriors.

A NOBLE DEATH
This famous statue, known as the *Dying Gaul*, presents a noble portrait of an injured Celtic chief as he endures suffering and awaits death. Battle wounds were a source of pride. A warrior who survived a fight might make his own injuries worse if they did not look very impressive.

MAKE A HELMET
You will need: bowl, PVA glue, water, newspaper, balloon, petroleum jelly, pair of compasses, felt-tip pen, card 17 cm x 8 cm, ruler, scissors, gold and bronze paint, paintbrushes, dowelling.

1 To make papier-mâché, fill the bowl with 1 part PVA glue to 3 parts water. Tear up the newspaper and soak the pieces in the glue and water mixture.

2 Blow up the balloon to the size of your head and cover with petroleum jelly. Build up papier-mâché layers on the top and sides of the balloon.

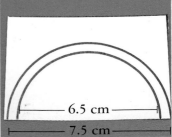

6.5 cm

7.5 cm

3 Use compasses to draw a semicircle on the card 7.5 cm in diameter. In the same way, draw another semicircle 6.5 cm in diameter inside the first.

WARRIOR ON WHEELS

After around 450BC, Celtic warriors were buried in lightweight, two-wheeled chariots, just like the chariots they drove into battle. Their weapons and drinking bowls were arranged beside them as well. This warrior's grave was discovered in northern France.

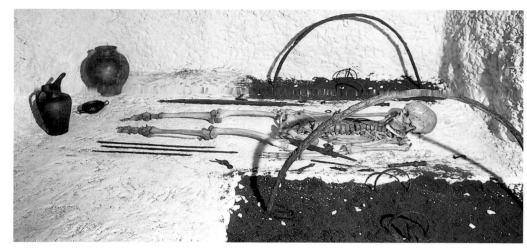

BRAVE SACRIFICE

A Celtic warrior commits suicide after killing his wife. This marble statue was created after the Gauls (migrating Celts from France) had been defeated by King Attalus I of Pergamon, Asia Minor, in 230BC. Roman writers reported that the Celts would choose death rather than spend the rest of their lives in captivity, or suffering from the dishonour of defeat.

HALLSTATT HELMET

This pointed metal helmet was found near Salzburg, in Austria, not far from the Hallstatt salt mines. It was buried in a warrior's grave during the La Tène era (450–50BC). Compare it with the helmet worn by the stone warrior in the statue on the opposite page.

The original helmet that inspired the design for your model was found in northern France. It was decorated with gold, which sparkled in the sun.

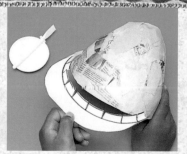

4 Draw lines at intervals in-between the two semicircles. Cut around the inner semicircle. Cut rounded corners off the top of the card, as shown.

5 When the papier-mâché helmet is dry, pop the balloon. Trim the helmet. Next, cut into the tabs on the peak. Glue the peak in position, as shown.

6 Paint all of the peak and helmet with gold paint and allow to dry. Then decorate with the bronze paint, using Celtic designs, as shown.

7 Finally, use the small piece of dowelling to add the finishing touches to your helmet. Place in a warm place until it is completely dry.

Head-hunting Raiders

RAIDING WAS AN ESSENTIAL PART of Celtic life. Bands of young, male warriors regularly rode off to attack and plunder neighbouring Celts or more distant foreign peoples. Raiding was the way for a man to win praise and to demonstrate his skill and bravery. It also increased his status within the community by attracting groups of loyal followers. These followers helped, supported and obeyed him in return for gifts and protection from attack.

Raids might last for a few hours or a few months, but their purpose was always the same. The aim was to win rich prizes such as captives, precious goods, animals or food. These were shared out by the raider among his followers, friends and relatives at a great feast. The more gifts the raider gave, the higher his prestige, and the more followers he could attract. The Celts also saw raiding as an enjoyable sport and as good training for war. On raids, Celtic warriors practised skills that would be useful on a battlefield, such as fighting with swords and spears, and horse riding.

Some historians think that the habit of making long-distance raids encouraged the Celts to start spreading across Europe. The Celtic migrations began in about 400BC, possibly because the Celts had run out of people to attack and lands to conquer nearer home.

SEVERED HEAD
After raids and battles, Celtic warriors might return home carrying the heads of enemies they had killed. They would nail these heads to the doors of their houses as trophies. It seems clear that heads had a special, religious or magic meaning for the Celts, but historians are not exactly sure what this was. Most think that, for the Celts, the head was the site of a person's spirit and power.

ON THE RUN
Made around 175BC, this Roman stone carving shows two Celtic warriors dropping the plunder they have seized on a raid. They are in a hurry to escape because they are being chased by angry enemies. The carving is part of a Roman monument celebrating the defeat of the Celts in northern Italy by Roman troops. The Roman stone-carver has shown the Celts as naked "barbarians". However, it is almost certain that the Celts went raiding with their clothes on.

A TERRIBLE SOUND

Before a fight, Celtic warriors performed war dances and battle chants, accompanied by loud, blaring carnyxes (war trumpets). You can see three carnyxes here, each one with a wolf-shaped head. Carnyxes were used more often in battles than on raids. Celtic raiders liked to swoop down on villages and farms in surprise attacks. In battle, the carnyx was used to cause panic among the enemy.

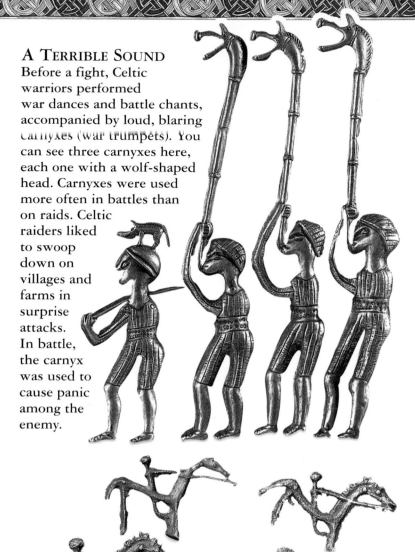

WAR PAINT

This modern reconstruction shows how a Celtic warrior might have looked as he prepared for a fight. Roman writers reported that the Celts painted or tattooed their bodies with typical Celtic patterns by using woad (a blue dye, made from plants). Today, no one knows what the patterns meant, but Celtic warriors probably believed that they gave them protection, or extra, magic powers.

RIDING TO RAID

The Celts were expert horse riders, and horses were among their most treasured possessions. These little lead figures were made in south Austria around 650BC. They show Celtic horsemen riding to a raid. Horses were valued almost as highly as humans and were buried respectfully when they died.

PURE GOLD

These three beautiful gold torcs were made by the Celts in Britain around 50BC. They were worn around the neck by rich men and women. The Celts hoped to seize such treasures when they went on raids. Celtic chieftains shared the captured goods among their followers. They might also give a share as an offering to the gods.

On Land and Sea

CELTIC IDEAS, technologies and designs spread across a wide area, from the borders of central Asia to the shores of the Atlantic Ocean. Travel in Celtic times was slow and difficult, compared with today. There were no paved roads, although the Celts did build causeways of wood across marshy ground. Overland journeys were made on foot or horseback, and only the wealthiest chiefs could afford to drive in chariots. For carrying heavy loads of farm produce, timber or salt, the Celts used wooden carts pulled by oxen. Celtic boats were built of wood, or of thick leather stretched across a wooden frame. They were powered by men rowing with oars, or by cloth or leather sails which trapped the wind.

It is highly unlikely that any individual traveller would have journeyed from one side of the Celtic lands to the other. However, many Celtic merchants, craftworkers, warriors and raiders made shorter journeys that brought them into contact with neighbouring peoples – both Celts and non-Celts. It seems likely that new ideas and inventions were spread in this way.

FAST CHARIOT
The early Celts of the Hallstatt era (750–450BC) buried heavy, four-wheeled wagons alongside important people. These wagons were slow and lumbering, useful only for carting heavy loads for short distances, or for ceremonial display. Between about 500BC and 400BC, lighter, faster, two-wheeled chariots, like the one on this coin, became popular in Celtic lands (and in Celtic burials, too). Some chariots were used for war, others were owned as status symbols by rich and powerful rulers.

FIT FOR A KING
Only the richest Celtic chiefs and warriors could afford to decorate their chariots with fine bronze and enamel fittings, such as this terret ring. It was used as a guide ring through which the horse's reins were passed.

HEAVY LOAD
This leather rucksack was worn by a Celtic workman about 2,800 years ago. It was found in the Hallstatt salt mines, and was used to carry blocks of rock salt along winding, underground passages that led to the entrance of the mine. This was a common way to carry heavy loads. Only the richest Celts could afford horses and wagons.

LAKE TRADE

One-person boats, such as this one, had deep, narrow hulls and upturned prows. They were made from planks of wood, and their design was based on the first-ever boats, which were hollowed out logs. They were used to carry cargo (including rock salt) across the Austrian lakes. This little wooden model is 10.5 cm long and was found in Austria.

SUMMIT PATHS

Long-distance tracks ran along the ridges of lowland hills, such as these chalk downs in southern England. The ground along these hill summits was usually well-drained, so people travelling on foot or on horseback did not sink into the mud. The elegant animal shape cut into this chalk hillside reminds us of the Celts' passion for horses. It may have been made in Celtic times, but some historians think that it is only about 1,000 years old.

MAGICAL PROTECTION

Wealthy Celtic warriors decorated their horse harnesses (which linked horses to their chariots) with elaborate metal plates. This harness plate would have been placed on the horse's forehead with two others, one on each side of the head. It is ornamented with a typical Celtic three-legged design. The number three was a sign of magic power for the Celts, and the owner of this plate may have hoped it would protect him and his horse from harm.

SAILING THE SEAS

This beautiful miniature boat, made of solid gold, is about 2,000 years old and was designed as an offering to the gods. It was found in County Derry in Ireland. Like full-sized Celtic boats, it has moveable oars, and a mast for a sail. The slats across the centre were seating for the boat's occupants. Celtic merchants and traders travelled around the coasts of western Europe in boats just like this one.

Weapons and Armour

CELTS RELIED ON THEIR STRENGTH – and their weapons – to survive in battle. Heavy Celtic swords were made of iron, and were used for cutting and slashing. They were carried in decorated scabbards made of bronze, wood or leather. Spears and javelins were lighter. They were used for stabbing at close quarters, or for throwing at an enemy many metres away. Round pebbles, hurled by cloth or leather slings, could also be deadly weapons. Archaeologists have found huge stockpiles of pebbles at Celtic hill forts. Wooden clubs were used by warriors to bludgeon their enemies in battle, but were also used for hunting birds.

For protection, Celtic warriors carried a long shield, usually made of wood and leather. Normally, Celtic men wore a thigh-length tunic over baggy trousers but, in battle, they often went naked except for a torc (twisted metal ring) around the neck, and a metal helmet. This nakedness was a proud display of physical strength – even the Celts' enemies admired their tall, muscular physique. The Celts believed that torcs gave magical protection. Their helmets, topped with magic crests, gave them extra height and made them look frightening.

CHAIN MAIL
The Celts sometimes used flexible chest coverings of chain mail in battle. Several burial sites have yielded actual chain mail such as that shown above, found in St Albans, England. However, most of the time, the Celts went into battle naked.

UNDRESSED TO KILL
This gold pin is decorated with the figure of a naked Celtic warrior, armed with sword, shield and helmet. One ancient writer described a Celtic warrior's weapons: "A long sword worn on the right side, and a long shield, tall spears, and a kind of javelin. Some also use bows and slings. They have a wooden warclub, which is thrown by hand with a range far greater than an arrow …"

MAKE A SHIELD
You will need: felt-tip pen, card 77 cm x 38 cm, scissors, ruler, pair of compasses, bottle top, bradawl, leather thongs, paper fasteners, sticky tape, drink carton lid, plasticine, PVA glue, paint, paintbrushes, dowling rod 75 cm long.

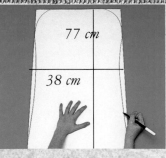

1 Draw a shield shape on to card. The shield should have rounded corners and curve in slightly on each of the long sides, as shown. Cut out.

77 cm
38 cm

2 Draw a vertical and a horizontal line through the centre of the shield. Add a large circle in the centre and two smaller circles either side, as shown.

29 cm
17 cm

3 With a felt-tip pen draw a typical Celtic design inside the circles, as shown. Use the bottle top and compasses to help you create your design.

SPANISH SHIELDS

The design of weapons and armour varied in different Celtic lands. These Celts are carrying small, round shields that originated in Spain. Shields were made from wood and leather. All Spanish warriors usually fought with a short, single-edged sword, called a *falcata*.

HANDY WEAPON

Daggers were used for fighting at close range. By the end of the Celtic era, when this dagger was made, their strong, sharp blades were usually forged from iron. They often had finely decorated hilts (handles), with scabbards (sheaths) fashioned from softer bronze. This Celtic dagger was found in the River Thames.

BRAIN GUARD

Helmets were usually made of iron, padded inside with cloth and covered on the outside by a layer of bronze. The high, domed shape protected the wearer's skull, and the peaked front kept slashing sword blows away from the eyes.

SHARP AND DEADLY

Celtic weapons were fitted with sharp metal blades, designed to cause terrible injuries. This bronze spear-point was made in Britain in about 1400BC, using techniques that were still employed by the Celts a thousand years later. Celtic metalworkers used moulds to make tools and weapons. Molten bronze was poured into the mould. Once the bronze object was cold and hard, rough edges were polished away, using coarse sand.

Shields were a speciality of craft workshops in southern England. A shield was one of a Celtic warrior's most prized possessions.

4 Use the bradawl to make two holes between the large and smaller circles, as shown. Thread the leather thongs through the holes.

5 With the bradawl, make small holes for the decorative paper fasteners. Push the paper fasteners through the holes and tape the ends on the back.

6 Stick the drink carton lid into the centre of the large circle. Roll long, thin plasticine snakes. Glue them along the lines of your decorative pattern.

7 Paint the front of the shield bronze. When dry, turn over and stick the dowling rod down the back. Use tape to secure. Tie the leather thongs.

War Against Rome

The ROMAN PEOPLE lived in southern Italy. At first, they were farmers, but gradually they built up a formidable army and began to conquer the surrounding lands. By the first century AD, they ruled over a vast empire. In order to conquer this empire, the Romans had to fight, especially against the Celts. The first major conflicts began soon after 400BC, when migrating bands of Celts from France arrived in northern Italy. Then, in 387BC, Celtic warriors attacked Rome. For the Romans, the Celts came to represent everything that was savage, barbarian and brutal – a great contrast, the Romans thought, to their own civilized ways of life. They determined to conquer the Celts and take over their lands. It took many years, but they succeeded.

Roman soldiers were impressed by the fast, two-horse chariots that Celtic chiefs rode into battle. However, the Romans soon discovered that most of the Celtic troops were no match for their well-organized, disciplined way of fighting, or for their short, stabbing swords. When the Celts saw their hero chiefs dead on the battlefield, the ordinary warriors panicked. They either hurled themselves recklessly towards the Romans, and were easily killed, or else retreated in confusion and despair.

ROMANS RIDING HIGH
This tombstone was carved as a memorial to a Roman soldier named Flavinus. He served as a standard-bearer in a cavalry regiment that was sent to enforce the Roman conquest of Britain in about AD50. It shows his horse trampling a Celtic warrior under its hoofs. The warrior has hair stiffened with lime to make him look more fierce. Despite their courage, Celtic foot soldiers had little chance of surviving a Roman cavalry charge.

CAPTIVE CELTS
Once captured by the Romans, Celtic men, women and children were either killed or sold as slaves. This painting dates from the 1800s and shows captive Celts in Rome. The artist has used their imagination to invent some details of the Celts' clothes and hairstyles. After success in war, the Romans paraded captured prisoners through the city.

TRIUMPH AND DEFEAT

Two Celts, captured and in chains, are depicted on a Roman triumphal arch. The arch was built around AD25 in southern France. It commemorates a Roman victory against the rebellious Gauls. The sculptor has shown the Gauls as the Romans imagined them, looking wild and ragged, and dressed in shaggy fur.

ENEMIES ON COINS

The Romans chose to show a Celtic warrior in his battle chariot on this Roman coin. They admired certain aspects of the Celtic civilization and were proud to have conquered such a people.

JULIUS CAESAR

Roman army commander Julius Caesar was very ambitious. He used his success against the Celts in France to help advance his political career in Rome. In 44BC, he declared himself "Dictator (sole ruler) for Life". He wrote a book describing his campaigns against the Celts. Although it paints a hostile picture of the Celtic people, Caesar's book has become one of the most important pieces of evidence about Celtic life. This silver coin shows Julius Caesar, represented as an elephant, crushing Gaul (France).

WALLED FRONTIER

In AD122, the Roman emperor, Hadrian, gave orders for a massive wall to be built across northern England. Its purpose was to mark the border between lands ruled by Rome and lands further north in Scotland, where Celtic chiefs still had power. Roman soldiers were stationed at forts built at intervals along the wall. They kept a look out for Celtic attackers, but also met, traded with, and sometimes married, members of the local Celtic population who lived and worked close to the wall.

Hilltop Forts

IN MANY CELTIC LANDS, houses, storerooms and cattle enclosures were surrounded by strong defensive walls. In uncertain times, when there were wars between Celtic tribes, or when Celtic lands were being attacked by outsiders, the Celts built hilltop forts for protection. In Ireland and Brittany, cliff castles were built, and in southern England, Germany and central Europe, there were hill forts. These hilltop forts also served as status symbols, to display the wealth and power of the tribe who built them.

To make a hill fort, teams of workers heaped up huge banks of earth around the summit of a hill, and topped them with strong wooden walls. The raised sites of the forts made it easy for defenders to see enemies advancing, and to hurl deadly spears and pebbles from within the forts' strong walls.

CLIFFTOP FORTS
Cliff castles were enclosures made of stone, built at the top of cliffs overlooking the sea. They were designed for defence, as status symbols, and perhaps as lookout points, as well. This "castle" is at Dun Aengus, on the Aran Islands, off the west coast of Ireland. The stones in the distance were placed around the castle to slow down attackers once they were in range of pebbles and slings.

WHICH WAY TO THE GATE?
The entrance to the hill fort of Maiden Castle, in southern England, could only be approached through this maze of curved earth banks. The banks were designed to slow down approaching enemies and confuse them. This gave the defenders inside the hill fort a chance to attack their enemies and drive them away. Archaeologists have found the skeletons of many Celtic warriors who died defending Maiden Castle, close to the entrance.

DEFENCES

The entrance to a hill fort was protected by a strong wooden gate, high ramparts (steep earth banks), and rows of sharp, pointed wooden stakes driven into the ground. Where the land was rocky, as here, the stakes were replaced by rows of sharp stones pointing upwards. Historians call this a *cheveux de frise*, the French words meaning "frizzy hair".

TALL TOWER

In Scotland, Celtic chiefs built massive brochs – tall, round stone towers. Brochs were probably originally safe places for people to shelter in wartime, but they soon became an important way of displaying a tribe's or a chieftain's power. The ruins of many Celtic brochs still survive today. This one is at Mousa, in the Shetland Isles, off the north coast of Scotland.

SCOTTISH HILL FORT

The hill forts of Dunagoil (left) and Little Dunagoil (centre) were used by the Celts. The ramparts were built of stone with timber-lacing. Following an attack on the fort, the timbers in the ramparts were set alight, causing the stones to heat up and vitrify (turn to glass).

ALMOST A TOWN

Towards the end of the Celtic era, some hill forts developed into large settlements, almost like towns. This artist's impression shows a typical *oppidum* (defended settlement) in Spain. The streets are laid out in a regular grid pattern, with closely packed blocks of houses. Merchants and craftsmen also had their workshops within the towns.

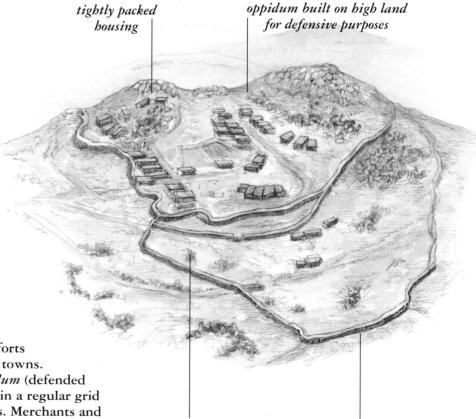

tightly packed housing

oppidum built on high land for defensive purposes

lower enclosures

surrounded by strong walls

Village Homes

ALTHOUGH MANY PEOPLE think of the Celts as fierce, wild warriors, most Celtic people were farmers who spent their lives in isolated farmsteads or small villages. The type of settlement depended on when and where it was built. The choice depended on local soils and farming methods, the social customs of the region, ancient traditions, and wartime dangers. Whatever their size, Celtic settlements were usually built close to reliable sources of essential supplies such as water, and fish and animals for hunting. Timber and meadowland for grazing livestock were important too. In addition, natural resources, such as copper and iron ore for smelting metals, clay for pottery making, and fertile soil for growing crops, were also vital.

FAMILY FARM

In lowland areas of Europe, Celtic families built villages of timber-framed roundhouses. Each family had a large house for living and several smaller buildings for sheltering animals and storing food. Grain was kept in pits underground, to protect it from rats.

COURTYARD HOMES

This aerial photograph shows the remains of a Celtic village at Chysauster, in Cornwall. It was built between AD1 and AD200. Each family had a house made up of several small stone chambers which were surrounded by circular walls of earth and stone. These walls created a safe courtyard where women could work, children could play, and animals could be sheltered at night. The Celts built their village houses out of locally available materials. For example, in rocky or mountainous regions such as Brittany, Cornwall or Scotland, rough lumps of stone were used to construct buildings.

MAKE A ROUNDHOUSE

You will need: string, felt-tip pen, brown card, scissors, ruler, 2 pieces of stiff white card 78 cm x 12 cm, PVA glue, masking tape, plasticine, rolling pin, straw, corrugated cardboard, 7 x dowling 45 cm long, bradawl.

1 Using the piece of string and a felt-tip pen draw a circle with a radius of 25 cm on the stiff brown card. Cut round the circle with the scissors.

2 Draw notches every 30 cm along the edges of the two pieces of white card. Cut in to the notches. Glue the two pieces of card together at one end.

3 Fit the wall to the base of your house, making sure the notches are along the top. Glue the wall in place and secure it with masking tape.

LAKE VILLAGE

In Scotland, the Celts built small artificial islands, called crannogs, in sheltered lochs (lakes) and rivers. They were connected to the shore by a narrow wooden bridge. Celtic families built their homes here, and surrounded them by wooden walls. They hoped they would be safer than in houses on dry land. This modern reconstruction shows a crannog on Loch Tay in central Scotland.

BUILDING MATERIALS

Some lowland Celtic houses were rectangular, others were built with circular walls and a conical roof. Both types were constructed around a framework of timber posts. The spaces in-between the wall timbers were filled with woven branches plastered with mud and clay. The roof timbers were covered with a layer of thatch, made from reeds or straw.

straw   *timber*

AN EXPERIMENT

Archaeologists experiment with different building techniques, such as this reconstructed wattle-and-daub wall, to find out more about how the Celts lived and worked.

CORACLE TRANSPORT

The Celts made short journeys across rivers and lakes in coracles (boats made of cattle hide stretched across a latticed wooden frame). Coracles were powered and steered with a single paddle. Most had space for only two or three people inside.

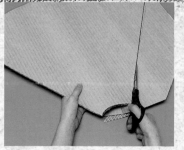

4 Roll out the plasticine into long sections 13 cm high. Sprinkle straw on to the plasticine and roll it in. Make enough sections to cover the wall.

5 Press the plasticine sections on to the wall until the whole wall is covered. Take care to keep the notches at the top of the wall visible.

6 Cut a large circle with a diameter of 91 cm from cardboard. Cut a small circle in the centre. Cut the large circle into sections 56 cm wide along the outer edge.

7 Glue straw on to these roof sections, starting on the outside edge and using three layers.

continues overleaf

Inside the Roundhouse

I**T WAS DARK AND SMOKY** inside a Celtic roundhouse, but quite comfortable. The thatched roof was a good insulator, keeping the house warm in the winter and cool in the summer. Celtic houses were heated by a wood or peat fire burning in a pit in the centre of the room. The hearth was the heart of the home, and the fire was kept burning day and night, all year round. Smoke from the fire drifted upwards, and escaped through the thatch.

There were no smoke-holes. Recently, archaeologists built a replica roundhouse. They found that leaving a hole in the roof to let smoke out led to sudden downdraughts, and risked setting the whole house on fire. Most houses had no windows, the only light coming from the fire or through the open door. The doorways were low, and protected by a tunnel-like porch to keep out wind and rain. The Celts owned little furniture, so people ate and slept on the ground. For warmth and comfort, they covered the pounded earth floor with heaps of animal skins or thick mattresses made of straw.

BULL BY THE HORNS
As logs burned on the hearth they were held in place by metal props known as firedogs. This is one of a set of four – one stood at each corner of the hearth. The Celts decorated their household goods with patterns and pictures. This iron firedog is topped with a bull's head decoration. The blacksmith has managed to give the bull a lively expression!

LOCAL LOOK
In different Celtic areas, houses were built to different designs. This Scottish roundhouse has a timber-framed thatched roof – both common local building materials.

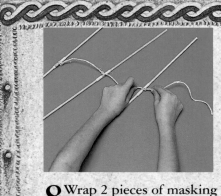

8 Wrap 2 pieces of masking tape 1 cm apart around the middle of 6 dowling sticks. Tie string betweem the tape. Allow 13 cm of string between each stick.

9 Take another dowling stick. Place it in the middle of the base of the house. Secure the stick in an upright position with plasticine.

10 Place the sticks for the roof structure over the house. Ask a friend to hold the centre, as shown, while you put sticks into the wall notches.

11 Use plasticine to hold the sticks in place in the wall notches. Then tie the top of the sticks securely together with a piece of string.

FIRES AND FOOD

As well as heating the roundhouse, the fire was also used for cooking. A large metal cauldron was suspended on heavy iron chains from cross beams in the roof. Animal skins, fish and meat could also be hung above the fire. Chemicals in the smoke helped to preserve them, and gave the smoked fish and meat a rich, tangy taste.

Roundhouses such as this were common in low-lying areas where wood was plentiful.

12 Add extra plasticine around the ends of the sticks and the wall notches. This will help to secure the roof structure firmly in place on the wall.

13 Tie together the ends of the string between the last two pieces of dowling. Keep the string taut to stop the sticks from collapsing.

14 Use the bradawl to make two holes on both edges at the top and bottom of each roof section. Thread a piece of string through each hole.

15 Use the ends of the string to tie the roof covering firmly on to the roof structure. Do this until the whole of the roof is covered.

Towns and Trade

Ｆｏｒ ｔｈｏｕｓａｎｄｓ ｏｆ ｙｅａｒｓ, different parts of Europe have been linked by long-distance trade. Well-known trade routes followed great river valleys, such as the Rhine, the Rhône and the Danube, or connected small ports along the coast, from Ireland to Portugal. As early as 600BC, traders from the Mediterranean claimed to have sailed through the Straits of Gibraltar and over the sea to the British Isles. After around 200BC, the Celts began to build fortified settlements as centres of government, craftwork and trade. Some grew up around existing hill forts or villages, others occupied fresh sites. The Romans called them *oppida*, the Latin word for town. Some of the oppida were very large. For example, Manching, in southern Germany, covered about 380 hectares, and its protective walls were 7 kilometres long.

WINE LOVERS
The Celts were very fond of wine, which they imported from Italy. Roman wine merchants transported their wine in tall pottery jars called amphorae. You can see four amphorae at the back of this picture.

HIGH VALUE
Celts learned how to make coins from the Macedonians, who lived in eastern Europe. The first Celtic coins were made of pure precious metals, such as gold and silver. They were made by stamping a metal disc between two dies (moulds).

SMALL CHANGE
In the second half of the Celtic era, coins were made from alloys (mixed metals) containing only a small amount of silver or gold. These coins were much less valuable than the earlier, pure metal ones. This alloy coin was made around 100BC in western France.

MAKE A WAGON
You will need: white card, ruler, felt-tip pen, scissors, balsa wood, PVA glue, masking tape, sandpaper, pair of compasses, paint and paintbrush, drawing pins, bradawl, leather thong.

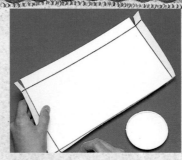

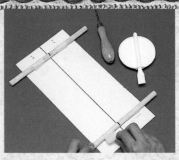

1 Take a piece of stiff white card measuring 29 cm x 16 cm. Using a ruler and felt-tip pen, draw lines 2 cm in from the edges of the card.

2 Make cuts in the corners of the card, as shown. Score along the lines and fold the edges up to make a box shape. This is the body of the wagon.

3 Take a piece of card 27 cm x 12 cm. Take two lengths of balsa wood 20 cm long. Stick them across the card, 4 cm in from the two ends.

KEY

♦ Iron
⊛ Tin
⌂ Amphorae (wine jars)
⚱ Amber
♈ Salt

Map labels: GREAT BRITAIN, MAITHABY, KEMMELBERG, UXISAME, MOSOMAGUS, STEINSBURG, LUTETIA, CONTIOMAGUS, RUBIN, MELUN, HERAPE, SEGODUNUM, ZAVIST, CENABUM, REINHEIM, MT LASSOIS, HEUNEBERG, CHASSEY, STUPAVA, ROANNE, CHATILLON-SUR-GLANE, LUGDONUM, MANTUA, ESTE, SPINA, CELTIBERIA (SPAIN AND PORTUGAL), MASSALIA, FELSINA

LONG-DISTANCE TRADE

Celtic merchants and craftworkers in different lands were linked together by a network of trade routes, leading north-south and east-west. Few traders would have travelled the length of any one route. Instead, merchants from different countries met at trading towns. Valuable goods might be bought and sold several times along a trade route before reaching their final owner.

TOWN WALLS

Oppida were surrounded by strong, defensive walls. These ruined ones are from a Celtic town in southern France. Within the walls, houses, streets and craft workshops were laid out in well-planned, orderly rows.

This model wagon is based on the remains of funeral wagons found buried in Celtic graves. The Celts used wagons that were more roughly made but easier to steer for carrying heavy loads.

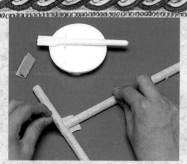

4 Take two sticks of balsa wood 26 cm and 11 cm long. Sand the end of the long stick to create a slight indent to fit against the short piece. Glue together.

5 Use the pair of compasses to draw four circles, each 10 cm in diameter, out of card. Next, carefully cut the circles out, as shown above.

6 Glue the box on to the piece of card. Attach the wheels to the balsa wood shafts by pressing a drawing pin through the centre of each wheel.

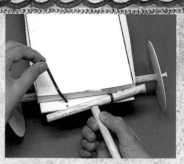

7 Make two holes in the front of the wagon with a bradawl. Thread the leather thong through the holes and attach the steering pole. Paint the wagon silver.

Fields and Animals

THE CELTS WERE FARMING PEOPLE. They cleared fields, planted crops, and bred livestock. They also fenced meadowland, and kept out their grazing animals until they had cut and dried the meadow grass to make hay for winter fodder. Celtic farmers used an iron-tipped plough, pulled by oxen, to turn over the soil in their fields and prepare the ground for planting. Seeds of grain were scattered by hand on ploughed land in early spring; the crops were ready to harvest in late summer or autumn. The Celts' most important crops were wheat, oats and barley, which could be cooked to make porridge, or ground into flour.

The most common farm animals were pigs, cattle, sheep and goats. As well as producing meat, animals provided milk (used to make butter and cheese), wool (spun and woven into cloth), and hides (which were tanned to make leather). The Celts also reared ducks and geese, for meat and eggs. Manure from animals and birds was used as a fertilizer on the fields. In some areas, Celtic farmers dug pits for marl (natural lime) to spread on their land. The lime helped to fertilize the soil and make the crops grow.

BULL'S EYE
Cattle were the most important farm animals in many Celtic lands. Oxen were used to pull carts and farm machinery, as well as for food. All cattle were highly prized, and were the main source of wealth for many farmers. Irish myths and legends tell of daring raids, when Celtic warriors galloped off to attack enemy farms and take all their cattle away.

SICKLE AND HOE
As crops grew in the fields, the Celtic farmer used a hoe (right) to keep the weeds down. The crops were harvested with a sharp, curved sickle (above). This hoe and sickle date from the La Tène era (450–50BC). Farming tools such as these were made by blacksmiths out of iron. Grain crops and hay were sometimes cut by an animal-drawn reaping machine, called a *vallus*. It was made of wood, with iron cutting blades.

WILD PAIR
The Celts raised pigs on their farms as well as hunting wild boar in the woods. Farm pigs were much smaller and thinner than European pigs today. They had long legs and stripy, bristly hair. In Celtic art, the boar was a symbol of great strength and power. These two little bronze pigs were probably made as offerings to the gods.

GRACEFUL GOOSE
This stone slab was carved in Scotland, in about AD450. It shows a goose turning round to preen its tail feathers. Geese were kept for their meat, eggs and grease. Goose grease could be rubbed on sore, dry skin, and used to soften and waterproof leather. Although the evidence has not survived, it seems likely that soft goose feathers were used to make warm bedding as well.

RARE BREED
The Soay sheep is an ancient breed that is rare today. It is similar to the sheep kept by Celtic farmers. It is small, nimble and hardy, and has long horns. Soay sheep do not need shearing because their fleece sheds naturally in summer. The wool can then be combed or pulled out by hand.

GOOD GRAINS
The Celts' main food crops were grains such as wheat, barley, oats and rye. These crops were harvested in late summer, heated over firepits to remove moisture, then stored in underground chambers (historians call them souterrains) for winter use.

wheat

barley

RIDGE AND FURROW
This photo shows ancient ridges and furrows in south-west England, created by later medieval farmers using techniques that may have been developed by the Celts. During the Celtic era, farmers began to move away from the light, well-drained soils on hilltops and slopes, clearing new fields on the heavier, wetter but more fertile land in valley bottoms. They invented heavy ploughs, fitted with wheels and pulled by oxen, to help cultivate this land.

Life on the Farm

MEN, WOMEN AND CHILDREN were all expected to play their parts in running a Celtic farm. It seems likely that both men and women worked in the fields. Men usually did the ploughing, but the women probably carried out tasks such as weeding the crops. Everyone helped at harvest time because it was vital to gather the grain as soon as it was ripe. There were countless other jobs that needed doing to keep the farm running smoothly, such as combing sheep, caring for sick animals, milking cows, collecting eggs, repairing thatched roofs, and fetching water. Along with all the other tasks around the farm, parents had to teach their children the skills they would need in adult life. Many Celtic parents sent their sons and daughters to live in other households until they were grown up. This was a way of making close bonds of friendship between families and tribes and also taught the children extra skills.

WRAPPED AND WARM
This carved stone statue of a baby wrapped in a blanket was made in Celtic France. Compared with today, it must have been difficult for mothers and grandmothers to keep young children clean, warm, dry and out of danger on a busy farm.

LOCKED UP
Keys like these were used to lock wooden chests containing valuable goods, such as the family's marriage wealth. This was the bride's dowry (money or treasure given by her father) plus an equal amount given by the husband on their wedding day. In some Celtic lands, wives had the right to inherit this if they outlived their husbands.

MAKE A POT

You will need: paper, bowl, PVA glue, water, balloon, petroleum jelly, card, pair of compasses, pencil, ruler, scissors, masking tape, cardboard core from roll of adhesive tape, pin, red and black paint, paintbrushes.

1 To make papier-mâché, tear paper or newspaper up into small strips. Fill a bowl with 1 part PVA glue to 3 parts water. Add the paper pieces and soak.

2 Blow up the balloon and cover in petroleum jelly. Cover the balloon in a layer of papier-mâché mixture. Leave to dry, then slowly build up more layers.

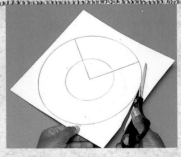

3 On the card draw a circle 20 cm in diameter. Draw a second circle inside it 9 cm in diameter. Mark off a quarter of both circles. Cut the large circle out.

DYED IN THE WOOL

The Romans reported that the Celts liked patterned, brightly coloured clothes. Sheep's wool was often dyed before being woven into cloth. Dyes were made from flowers, bark, berries, leaves or lichen boiled together with salt, crushed rock or stale urine. The wool was soaked in this mixture then boiled again, or left to soak for several hours.

sheep's wool   *lichen*

HAND-WOVEN

Many Celtic women made clothes and blankets from sheep's wool from their own farms. First, they cleaned and sorted the wool, then they spun it into thread. The thread was woven on an upright loom. Heavy weights kept the warp (vertical) threads straight while the weft (horizontal) thread was passed in-between.

PEDESTAL POTS

Celtic women made simple pottery bowls and dishes for use at home. Wealthy Celtic people could also afford elegant vases and jugs like these pedestal pots (pots with feet), made by expert craftworkers in towns.

BUTTER BUCKET

Wooden buckets such as this were used on many Celtic farms, but few have survived. This one was found buried in a bog in northern Scotland. It contained butter. The damp, airless conditions in the bog had stopped the wood rotting.

Decorate your pedestal pot with a swirling pattern in typical Celtic style. The Celts liked bright colours – the pot that inspired this model was originally bright red.

4 Cut a quarter of the outer circle and all of the inner circle out, as shown. The outer circle will be the pot base. Stick the ends together with tape.

5 Use the cardboard inner from a roll of adhesive tape to make the stem of the pot. Attach it to the card base with masking tape.

6 Burst the balloon with a pin. Cut the top end of the pot off evenly. Attach the base and stem to the bottom of the pot with masking tape.

7 Paint the whole pot with red paint, including the stem and neck. Then add the Celtic pattern, as shown above, in black paint.

37

Food and Drink

FOOD WAS VERY IMPORTANT TO THE CELTS. They enjoyed eating and drinking, and were not ashamed of getting drunk, or of rowdy behaviour. They did not, however, approve of people getting too fat. Roman writers reported that Celtic warriors were ordered not to let out their belts, but to lose weight, when clothes around their waists became too tight! The Celts produced most of their own food on their farms. They needed to buy only items such as salt (used to preserve meat and fish), and luxury goods such as wine. They also hunted and fished for many wild creatures, and gathered wild fruits, nuts, herbs and mushrooms from meadows and forests. Celtic families were famous throughout Europe for their hospitality to strangers. It was their custom to offer food and drink to any visitor, and not to ask who they were or where they were from until the end of the meal.

HANGING CAULDRON
Meals for large numbers of people were cooked in a big cauldron. This bronze cauldron, iron chain and hook were made around 300BC in Switzerland. A cauldron could also be used for boiling water, heating milk to make cheese, or brewing mead.

CELTIC CASSEROLE
Meat, beans, grains and herbs were stewed in a covered clay pot. The pot could be placed directly on glowing embers or (as shown here) balanced on a hearthstone. This stone hearth, with a hollow pit for the fire, was found at an oppidum (Celtic town) in France.

MAKE SOME OATCAKES
You will need: 225 g oatmeal, 75 g plain flour, salt, baking soda, 50 g butter, water, bowl, sieve, wooden spoon, small saucepan, heat-resistant glass, board, rolling pin, baking tray, wire tray.

1 Preheat the oven to 220°C/425°F/Gas 7. Put 225 g of oatmeal into a large bowl. Add 75 g of plain flour. Sieve the flour into the bowl.

2 Next add 1 teaspoon of salt to the oatmeal and flour mixture. Mix all the ingredients in the bowl together well using a wooden spoon.

3 Add a quarter teaspoon of bicarbonate of soda (baking soda) to the oatmeal and flour mixture. Mix it in well and then put the bowl to one side.

GRINDING GRAIN

All kinds of grain were ground into flour using hand-powered querns (mills) like this one. The grains were poured through a hole in the top stone. This stone was then turned round and round. The grains became trapped and were crushed between the top and bottom stones, spilling out of the quern sides as flour.

FRUITS FROM THE FOREST

The Celts liked eating many of the same fruits and nuts that we enjoy today. However, they had to go and find them growing on bushes and trees. We know that the Celts ate fruit because archaeologists have found many seeds and pips on rubbish heaps and in lavatory pits at Celtic sites.

wild cherries

apples

hazelnuts

blackberries

OUT HUNTING

Celtic men went hunting and fishing for sport, and also as a way of finding food. This stone carving, showing a huntsman and his dogs chasing deer, was made around AD800 in Scotland. By then, Celtic power had declined, but many Celtic traditions persisted.

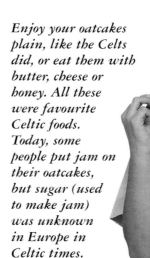

Enjoy your oatcakes plain, like the Celts did, or eat them with butter, cheese or honey. All these were favourite Celtic foods. Today, some people put jam on their oatcakes, but sugar (used to make jam) was unknown in Europe in Celtic times.

4 Next, melt the butter in a small saucepan over a low heat. Make sure that it does not burn. Add the melted fat to the oat and flour mixture.

5 Boil some water. Place a little of the water in a mug or heat-resistant glass. Gradually add the boiled water to the mixture until you have a firm dough.

6 Turn the dough out on to a board sprinkled with a little oatmeal and flour. Roll the dough until it is about 1 cm thick. Cut the dough into 24 circles.

7 Place the circles of dough on a greased baking tray. Bake in the oven for 15 minutes. Allow the oatcakes to cool on a wire tray before serving.

A Celtic Feast

CELTIC STORIES AND POEMS often describe splendid feasts, in which food is served all day and all night. These feasts were far more than occasions for eating and drinking. They were a way of bonding together all the most important men in a community, of displaying wealth and power, of settling quarrels between warriors, and of deciding status within the tribe. Feasts were for men only, although women often cooked and served the food. The host and his guests, warrior heroes or noblemen, sat in a circle, with the honoured guest (usually the bravest hero) in the seat of honour. The assembled company might be entertained by a musician, who composed songs in their praise. The honoured guest was served with the choicest cut of meat (from the thigh), called the champion's portion. But if another guest felt he was braver, then he would claim the portion, and the two would fight.

DRINKING DEEP
A Celtic warrior on horseback drains the last drops of drink from a horn in this carving. Huge drinking horns, made from real ox horn or iron, were used by Celtic chieftains. They were symbols of a chief's power.

WINE CUP
At a feast, wine and mead were served in huge buckets or bowls then poured into individual cups. This bronze cup was made in the British Isles in about AD40. Its handle is shaped like a waterbird.

PLAY THE GAME
You will need: modelling clay, rolling pin, wooden board, ruler, clay cutting tool or pencil, paint and paintbrushes.

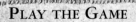

1 Roll out the clay using the board and rolling pin. The finished slab should measure about 20 cm x 15 cm, and be about 1.5 cm thick.

2 Using a cutting tool, mark out a grid. It should have seven horizontal and seven vertical lines. Make a small circular pit in the centre with a pencil.

3 Leave the board in a warm place to dry. Cover the slab with dilute grey paint, as shown. Then leave the board in a warm place to dry.

IRON BLADES

The Celts ate with knives, spoons or their fingers, as forks were not invented until the Middle Ages. These iron meat-cutting knives were made in Germany in about AD50. Their blades are similar in shape to many cooking knives today. For comfort, their handles might have been bound with string (woven from plant fibres) or leather thongs.

MEAD AND ALE

The Celts brewed two of their favourite alcoholic drinks at home, using local ingredients. Mead was made from honey and herbs, and ale was made from barley and flavoured with heather. Grapes for making wine did not grow well in many Celtic lands, so wine was imported.

grapes

honey

heather

GAMING PIECES

The Celts enjoyed playing games and making bets. These little glass counters were made by Celtic craftworkers and were used for gambling, or playing board games.

No one knows exactly what board games the Celts played. You could use your counters to play draughts, or invent a game of your own.

BUCKET FOR BANQUETS

This finely decorated bronze bucket was made in about 100BC. It was probably used for mixing wine with water before offering it to guests. In wine-growing countries, wine was always diluted with water, so that guests would not get too drunk!

4 Using your fingertips and palms, mould counters, as shown. The counters should have flat bottoms. Make 12 counters.

5 Divide the counters into threes. Paint the counters in the first group with the same swirly design. Choose a different combination of colours for each group.

6 Now combine the pieces to make two separate sets with different patterns. Place the counters at either end of the grid, as shown.

7 The Celts probably played on the intersections rather than the squares. The central circle may have been a safe haven where the pieces cannot be taken.

41

Celtic Clothes

THE CELTS LOVED FINE CLOTHES AND RICH JEWELS. The Greek geographer, Strabo, wrote about the appearance of the Celts: "They wear gold jewellery, torcs on their necks, and bracelets on their arms and wrists, while people of high rank wear dyed garments ornamented with gold." Celtic women's clothes were long and loose. Depending on the season, they might be light linen, or thick, warm wool, but the style was usually the same – a sleeveless tunic over a long dress, with a lightweight shift (a simple undergarment) beneath. Over these clothes, women wore a shawl or a cloak that fastened at the shoulder.

At this time, most men wore tunics, but Celtic men were unusual because they wore trousers. This was a style they had copied from nomads from beyond the eastern borders of Europe. Like the Celts, the nomads were keen horse riders, and the Celts found that trousers were more practical for riding than tunics. They were also much warmer in winter. Over their trousers, Celtic men wore a short tunic and a cloak. Jewellery was similar for both women and men. Only wealthy people could afford gold, but ordinary people still liked to wear bracelets and necklaces of cheaper metals, such as bronze, and polished stone or pottery beads. Chiefs often rewarded their best warriors with rich gifts of fine gold arm-rings.

FLOWING ROBES
This Roman statue shows a Celtic woman from northern Italy during a battle. She is dressed in a knee-length tunic worn over a long, full-skirted dress. Over her left arm she has draped a cloak or shawl, and there is a wide, leather belt around her waist. She is also wearing a bracelet around her right wrist.

CELTIC CHECKS
The Celts were fond of bright colours and checked patterns. This fragment of brown and green check cloth (lying on top of a modern reconstruction) is one of the oldest pieces of fabric in the world. It was made from hand-spun wool and coloured with plant dyes. The cloth was found in the Hallstatt salt mines, and was made about 2,800 years ago. Spinning, dyeing and weaving cloth was women's work.

FOR WINTER WEATHER

A Celtic craftworker designed this hooded cape to keep the wearer warm in winter time. It is woven from wool, and has a band of decorative weaving and a long, tasselled fringe around its lower edge. It was made in the Orkney Islands, off the north coast of Scotland, between about AD250 and AD600.

SALTED SHOES

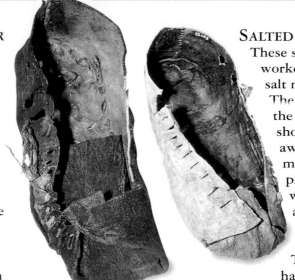

These shoes were worn by workers at the Hallstatt salt mines around 500BC. The salty conditions in the mines stopped the shoes from rotting away. The shoes are made from a single piece of calf-skin which was wrapped around the foot with the hair on the inside for warmth. These shoes would have been held in place by long laces, rather like those used in modern trainers.

TUNIC AND TROUSERS

This Celtic musician from Spain is comfortably dressed in tunic, trousers and short cloak. He is wearing shoes similar to the ones shown in the picture above. His short, thick hair is brushed back from the forehead in a favourite Celtic style. Few Celtic men let their hair grow very long, but cut it off about level with the bottom of their ears.

PRETTY WOMAN

The beautiful princess Etain is depicted in this painting from the 1800s. She was described in ancient Irish legends as the most beautiful woman in the world. These descriptions give us some clues of the Celts' ideas about beauty. According to the legends, Etain had bright eyes, like flowers, dark eyebrows, like a beetle's wing, and white teeth, like pearls. Her long hair was plaited into braids, and her cheeks were pink, like foxgloves.

Proud and Beautiful

CELTIC MEN AND WOMEN took great pride in their appearance because it made people admire them – and it could be useful. The Romans reported that different groups of men within Celtic society cut their hair and shaved their faces in different styles. This made it clear how important they were. Legends told that warriors who did not have blonde hair (preferred by the Celts) sometimes bleached their hair with a mixture of urine and wood-ash. Before a battle, they might also make their hair stand up on their heads like a crest, using a similar mixture. They hoped this would scare their enemies. Looking good could also work magic. The Celts wore gold torcs because they had special protective powers. For the same reason they sometimes painted or tattooed their bodies with a dark blue dye, called woad.

A CHIEFTAIN'S MOUSTACHE
This stone carving of a Celtic chieftain was made around 100BC in Czechoslovakia. Celtic chieftains shaved their beards but grew long, drooping moustaches. Like the torc this chieftain is wearing around his neck, moustaches were a sign of high status.

POLISHED MIRROR
Mirrors made of polished metal were among Celtic women's most treasured possessions. Craftworkers in Britain became especially skilled at making them between around 100BC and AD100. This mirror is made of bronze. The back is covered with a swirling design and the handle is carefully shaped to match.

MAKE A BROOCH

You will need: rolling pin, modelling clay, board, clay tool, pencil, sandpaper, paints, paintbrush, safety pin, sticky tape.

1 Roll out the modelling clay on a board to about 15 cm x 15 cm. Copy a dragon shape on to the clay, using the finished brooch on the next page as a guide.

2 Cut the brooch shape out of the clay. With the modelling tool, start to draw some of the detail, as shown, into the centre of your brooch.

3 Cut the interior hole out of the brooch. Next add the dragon's two faces and more decorative patterns using a modelling tool, as shown.

ADORNMENT AND CLEANLINESS

The Celts made several different beauty preparations from natural materials. They mixed stale urine and wood-ash to make a kind of soap. Slaked lime (made by burning crushed limestone) was also mixed with water to bleach and stiffen their hair. They also made a deep blue dye to paint patterns on their skin from woad, a plant related to flax.

soap

woad

lime

ALMOST A RING

The shape of this type of brooch is known as penannular (almost a ring). They were worn on the shoulder to keep heavy cloaks in place. This brooch is made of silver and gold, and is studded with pieces of glass and amber.

HEAVY TO WEAR

Large bronze rings, similar to this one, have been found around the ankles of skeletons in Celtic graves. They must have been heavy to wear, but looking good was more important than comfort!

BRAIDED HAIR

This gold and silver head of a goddess appears on one of the most famous Celtic objects – the Gundestrup Bowl. The bowl was made in eastern Europe in around 50BC. The artist has shown a tiny human serving-woman plaiting the goddess's hair in a popular Celtic style.

The brooch that inspired this design was made in Britain in around AD100. Brooches like this one are sometimes called dragon brooches.

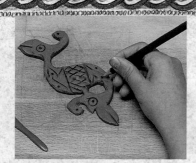

4 Finish the patterns on your brooch with the sharp end of a pencil. Leave the brooch in a warm place, such as an airing cupboard, to dry.

5 Next, gently hold the brooch in one hand. With your other hand, sand the edges carefully until they are almost completely smooth.

6 Paint the brooch with a light blue background colour. Add dark blue and white decorations. Put the brooch to one side until it is completely dry.

7 Stick the safety pin on to the back of your brooch with a small piece of sticky tape, as shown. Pin the brooch on your T-shirt or top.

Metalworking

METALWORKERS WERE SOME of the most important people in Celtic society. They made many of the items that Celtic people valued most, from bronze and iron swords to beautiful gold jewellery. It took several years to learn all the necessary skills, first to produce metal from raw nuggets or lumps of ore, and then to shape it. Metalworkers probably began their training very young, but even skilled workers seemed to have been ready to learn. Patterns and techniques invented in one part of the Celtic world were quickly copied and spread to other parts. Celtic metalworkers excelled in several different techniques. Heavy objects were cast from solid bronze, using a clay mould. Iron was heated in a very hot fire to soften it, then hammered into shape. Thin sheets of silver and bronze were decorated with repoussé (pushed out) designs. The designs were sketched on to the back of the metal, then gently hammered to create raised patterns.

PROTECTION FOR THE HAND

This bronze shield-boss was made in southern Britain between about 200BC and 10BC. A boss is the metal plate that was fixed to the centre of a shield to protect the hand of the person holding it. This example is decorated with a raised pattern of leaves and bird heads, using the repoussé technique.

TOOLS OF THE TRADE

Many bronze items, such as this horse's bit (left) and harness-ring (far left), were made by pouring molten metal into clay moulds, then leaving it to cool and become solid. You can also see fragments of the clay moulds, and the little crucible used for melting the bronze (top left).

MAKE A MIRROR

You will need: pair of compasses, pencil, ruler, stiff gold mirror card, scissors, tracing paper, pen, modelling clay, board, gold paint, paintbrush, PVA glue.

1 With the compasses, draw a circle 22 cm wide on to gold card. Cut out. Use this circle as a template to draw a second circle on to gold card.

2 Cut out the second gold circle. Draw another circle on tracing paper. Fold the piece of tracing paper in two and draw a Celtic pattern in pencil.

3 Lay the tracing paper on to one of the circles. Trace the pattern on to half of the gold circle, then turn the paper over and repeat. Go over the pattern with a pen.

FROM EARTH AND SEA

The most valuable materials for metalworking were difficult and sometimes dangerous to find. Silver ore was dug from mines underground, or from veins in rocks on the surface. Miners searched for nuggets of gold in gravel at the bottom of fast-flowing streams. Swimmers and divers hunted for coral that grew on little reefs in the Mediterranean Sea.

bronze ore

coral

gold nuggets

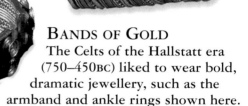

BANDS OF GOLD

The Celts of the Hallstatt era (750–450BC) liked to wear bold, dramatic jewellery, such as the armband and ankle rings shown here. They were found in a tomb in central France. Both the armband and the ankle rings were made of sheets of pure gold and twisted gold wire which were carefully hammered and soldered together.

DELICATE DESIGN

This button hole was created using the lost wax method of casting. The shape of the piece was modelled in beeswax, then the fine details were added. The wax model was covered with a thick layer of clay. Then the clay-covered model was heated, and the wax ran out. Finally, molten gold was poured into the space where the wax had been.

TOOLS OF THE TRADE

These little bone spatulas (knives for scooping and spreading) were used by metalworkers to add fine details to the surface of wax models when casting bronze objects using the lost wax process.

The bronze on a Celtic mirror would have polished up so that the owner could see his or her reflection in it.

4 Roll out several snakes of modelling clay and sculpt them into a handle, as shown here. The handle should be about 15 cm long and 9 cm wide.

5 Leave the modelling clay to dry. Then paint one side of the handle with gold paint. Leave to dry, then turn over and paint the other side.

6 Stick the two pieces of mirror card together, white side to white side. Glue the handle on to one side of the mirror.

Arts and Crafts

Art was essential to the Celts. Beautiful objects were not only good to look at, they also carried important messages about their owner's wealth and power. Their designs might have a magic or religious meaning to protect people from harm, or to inspire warriors setting off to war. The Celts were skilled at many different arts and crafts. Many examples of their pottery, glass, enamel, metalwork and jewellery remain for us to admire. From written descriptions of their clothes, we also know that the Celts were skilled weavers and dyers, although few pieces of cloth have survived.

We do not know much about the people who made these fine objects. They may have been free and independent, or the skilled slaves of wealthy families. However, from the archaeological evidence that survives we do know that, towards the end of the Celtic period, many Celtic craftworkers worked in oppida (fortified towns) instead of in country villages, as before.

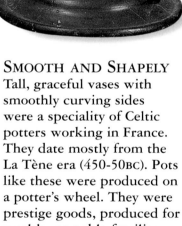

Smooth and Shapely
Tall, graceful vases with smoothly curving sides were a speciality of Celtic potters working in France. They date mostly from the La Tène era (450-50BC). Pots like these were produced on a potter's wheel. They were prestige goods, produced for wealthy or noble families.

Angular Art
During the Hallstatt era (750-450BC), Celtic potters decorated their wares with spiky, angular designs like the patterns on this pottery dish. After about 500BC, when compasses were introduced into Celtic lands from countries near the Mediterranean Sea, designs based on curves and circles began to replace patterns made up of angles and straight lines.

Make a Torc
You will need: board, modelling clay, ruler, string, scissors, PVA glue and brush, gold or bronze paint, paintbrush.

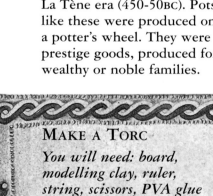

1 On the board, roll out two lengths of modelling clay, as shown. Each length should be approximately 60 cm long and about 1 cm thick.

2 Keeping the two lengths of clay on the board, plait them together. Leave about 5 cm of the clay unplaited at either end, as shown.

3 Make loops out of the free ends by joining them together. Dampen the ends with a little water to help join the clay if necessary.

PRECIOUS BOX
This gold and silver box belonged to St Columba. It was made in Ireland and was designed to hold Christian holy relics. After the saint's death, it was kept as a lucky talisman, and carried into battle by Scottish armies. They believed that St Columba would bring them victory.

GLASS JEWELS
The Celts used glass in different ways to create beautiful objects. Glass was made from salt, crushed limestone and sand, and coloured by adding powdered minerals. Craftworkers melted and twisted different coloured strands together to make jewel-like beads. Glass was also used as enamel, a thin, transparent layer bonded to metal underneath.

manganese
glass
cobalt
lead

MAKING WAVES
The sides of this pot are decorated with a moulded pattern of overlapping waves. The pot has survived unbroken from the La Tène era over 2,000 years ago. It was found in France and it is made from fired clay. Celtic potters built elaborate kilns to fire (bake) their pots at high temperatures.

ELEGANT ENAMEL
This bronze plaque is decorated with red and yellow enamel. It was made in southern Britain around 50BC and was designed to be worn on a horse's harness.

Torcs were status symbols for the Celtic people. They were made from precious metals such as iron, bronze and gold.

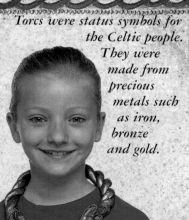

4 With the ruler, measure an opening between the two looped ends. The ends should be about 9 cm apart so that the torc fits easily around your neck.

5 When the torc is semi-dry, cut two pieces of string about 8 cm long. Use the string to decorate the torc's looped ends. Glue the string in place.

6 Allow the clay to dry completely. When it is hard, cover all the clay and string with gold or bronze paint. Leave to dry.

Messages in Stone

THERE WERE SEVERAL DIFFERENT Celtic languages, but no Celtic alphabet. To write something down, the Celts had to borrow other peoples' scripts. Sometimes they used Greek letters, sometimes Latin (the Romans' language). In the British Isles, a script known as Ogham was based on the Latin alphabet, but used straight lines instead of letters. Celtic craftworkers used all these different ways of writing to carve messages in stone. Their inscriptions might commemorate an important event, or a person who had died, or be a proud symbol of a leader's power. Craftworkers also decorated stones with beautiful patterns, sometimes copied from jewellery and metalworking designs. In some parts of the Celtic world, standing stones and lumps of rock were carved with special symbols. Historians think that these picture-carvings were designed to increase respect for powerful leaders, and for the gods.

STANDING STONE

Tall, carved standing stones were a special feature of Celtic lands in north-west France and Ireland. Archaeologists are not sure why they were put up or decorated, but they probably marked boundaries or holy sites. This stone comes from Turoe, in Ireland.

PRACTICE MAKES PERFECT

Before using precious metals such as gold, or starting to chip away at hard, valuable materials such as stone, craftworkers made sketches and worked out patterns on little pieces of bone. These bone fragments, marked with compass designs, were found in Ireland. They belonged to craftworkers from around AD50.

MAKE AN OGHAM STONE

You will need: modelling clay, board, rolling pin, ruler, modelling tool, sandpaper, white paint, paintbrush, green card, scissors, PVA glue.

1 Roll out the modelling clay to make a strip roughly 33 cm long, 5 cm wide and 3 cm thick. Carefully shape the top as shown.

2 Take the modelling tool and make a hole in the top end of the strip. This tall "holed" Ogham stone is based on one in southern Ireland from AD400.

3 These are some of the Ogham letters.

B
L
F
S
N

H
D
T
C
Q

M
G
NG
STR
R

A
O
U
E
I
EA

ON LIVING ROCK

This rough slab of stone is decorated with a Pictish carving of a wild boar. It was found in Dunadd, Scotland. Archaeologists have many theories as to why it was carved. It may have been a memorial to a dead leader or a notice announcing an alliance between friendly clans. An alternative view is that it was a tribal symbol, put up as a proud boast of the local peoples' power or a sign of a local chieftain's land.

THE CELTS LIVE ON

The Picts were a mysterious people who lived in Scotland from about AD79 to 900. They were descended from Celtic people and they continued many of the Celts' customs and traditions. In particular, they carved picture-symbols and Ogham letters on stone slabs, in caves and on lumps of rock. This stone monument, from Orkney, Scotland, shows three warriors and various other common Pictish symbols.

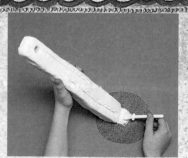

ALL CHANGE

Many tall, carved stones had religious power for the Celts. When Christian missionaries arrived in Celtic lands, they sometimes decided to make old carved stones into Christian monuments. They hoped this might help people understand that the Christian God was more important than the old Celtic ones. This stone is at Oronsay in the Orkney Islands off the north-east coast of Scotland.

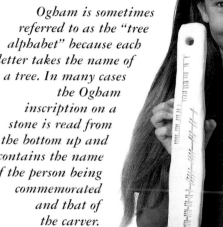

Ogham is sometimes referred to as the "tree alphabet" because each letter takes the name of a tree. In many cases the Ogham inscription on a stone is read from the bottom up and contains the name of the person being commemorated and that of the carver.

4 Ogham writing is done as a series of lines or notches scored across a long stem. Use the alphabet in step 3 to help you write something on your stone.

5 Ogham inscriptions are often found on memorials featuring a person's name. You could try writing your name on your model Ogham stone.

6 Sand the modelling clay gently to remove any rough edges. Then paint one side of your stone. Leave to dry, turn over and paint the other side.

7 Cut a circular base out of green card, roughly 14 cm wide. Glue the bottom of your stone on to the base, as shown. Now leave the stone to dry.

Bards and Musicians

THE CELTS ENJOYED MUSIC, poems and songs as entertainment, and for more serious purposes. Music accompanied Celtic warriors into battle and made them feel brave. Poems praised the achievements of a great chieftain or the adventures of bold raiders, and recorded the history of a tribe. Dead chieftains and heroes, and possibly even ordinary people, too, were mourned with sad laments. On special occasions, and in the homes of high-ranking Celts, poems and songs were performed by people called bards.

Roman writers described the many years of training to become a bard. Bards learned how to compose using all the different styles of poetry, and memorised hundreds of legends and songs. They also learned how to play an instrument, and to read and write, although most Celtic music and poetry was never written down. Becoming a bard was the first step towards being a druid (priest).

HOLY MUSIC
We do not know what part music played in Celtic religious ceremonies, but it was probably important. This stone statue shows a Celtic god playing a lyre. The Celts believed that religious knowledge, and music, was too holy to be written down. Sadly, this means that many Celtic poems and songs have been lost for ever.

GRACEFUL DANCER
Naked dancing girls may have entertained guests at important feasts. This little bronze statue, just 13cm high, dates from around 50BC. The Celts enjoyed dancing, and from the evidence of this statue it seems likely that their dances were quite wild in their movements.

MAKE A HARP
You will need: card 39 cm x 49 cm, pencil, ruler, scissors, cardboard 39 cm x 49 cm , felt-tip pen, paints, paintbrushes, bradawl, coloured string, paper fasteners.

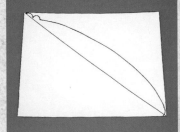

1 On the piece of card, draw a diagonal line from corner to corner. Draw a second, gently curving line, shaped at one end, as shown .

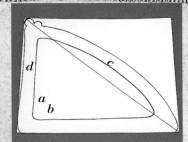

2 Draw two lines (*a* and *b*), 4.5 cm in from the edge of the paper. Join them with a curved line *c*. Finally add a curved line *d* parallel to *a*, as shown.

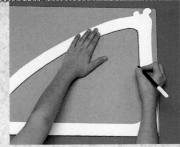

3 Cut out the harp shape. Place it on cardboard. Carefully draw round it with a felt-tip pen both inside and out. Cut the cardboard harp out.

HARPIST
This harpist is pictured on the Dupplin Cross, from Scotland. The harp itself is large and triangular in shape. It was placed on the ground and held between the harpist's knees. Such harps were popular at the end of the Celtic period.

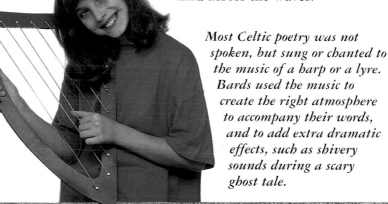

RELIGIOUS MUSIC
Musicians are shown playing at a religious ceremony on this stone carving from Scotland, dating from around AD900. The bottom panel shows a harpist plucking the strings of his harp, while a fellow musician plays a pipe. In the foreground is a drum, possibly made from a barrel with a skin stretched over it.

INSPIRED BY A DREAM
While a Celtic bard sleeps, he dreams of a beautiful woman from the world of the spirits. She will be the subject of his next song. Dreams and visions were a common theme in many ancient Celtic poems and legends. For example, Oisin, son of the great hero Finn MacCool, ran away with Niamh of the Golden Hair. Niamh was a spirit who appeared to Finn in a dream and invited him to come to a magic land across the waves.

Most Celtic poetry was not spoken, but sung or chanted to the music of a harp or a lyre. Bards used the music to create the right atmosphere to accompany their words, and to add extra dramatic effects, such as shivery sounds during a scary ghost tale.

4 Glue the one side of the card and and one side of the cardboard. Stick them together. Paint the harp brown and leave it in a warm place to dry.

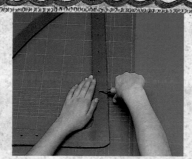

5 Use a bradawl to make holes approximately 5 cm apart along the two straight sides of the harp. These will be the holes for the strings.

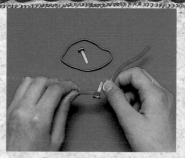

6 Cut a length of string 40 cm long. Cut 7 more pieces of string each 5 cm shorter than the last. Tie a paper fastener to both ends of each string.

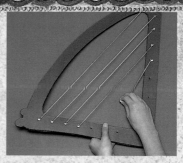

7 Push the paper fasteners in to the harp frame so that the strings lie diagonally across the harp. Adjust the strings so that they are stretched tightly.

53

Gods and Spirits

THERE ARE MANY surviving traces of Celtic religion, in descriptions by Roman writers, in carvings and statues, in place names, in collections of religious offerings, and in myths and legends. Yet there are many things we do not know or fully understand about Celtic beliefs. This is because the Celts believed that holy knowledge was too important to be written down. It seems almost certain, however, that the Celts worshipped gods who protected the tribe and gave strength in war, and goddesses who protected homes and brought fertility. The gods were associated with the sky, and the goddesses with the earth. Gods and spirits controlled the elements and natural forces, such as water and thunder, and they were given different names in different parts of the Celtic world. Both gods and goddesses were worshipped close to water and in groves of trees. Rich offerings were left for them. The Celts believed that dreadful things would happen if they did not make sacrifices of their most valuable possessions, including living things, to the gods.

GIFT TO THE GODS
This wooden statue is carved to look like a man wearing a Celtic hooded cloak. It was found at the source of the River Seine, in France. Small carvings like this were used to send messages to the gods.

HANDS HELD HIGH
From the Gundestrup bowl, this bearded god holds his hands up. Such a gesture may have been used by druids (Celtic priests) when praying. The clenched fists are a sign of power.

MAKE THE GUNDESTRUP BOWL
You will need: plastic bowl, silver foil, scissors, cardboard strip 12 cm x 84 cm, felt-tip pen, plasticine, PVA glue, double-sided tape, bradawl, paper fasteners.

1 Find a plastic bowl that measures about 26 cm in diameter across the top. Cover the bowl on the inside and outside with silver foil.

2 Use the pair of scissors to trim any excess foil, as shown. Ensure you leave enough foil to turn over the top edge neatly.

3 Divide the card into six sections. Leave 3 cm at the end of the card. Draw a god figure in each section. Make a plasticine version of the figure. Glue it on top.

BURIED IN A BOG

The remains of this Celtic man were found in a peat bog in northern England. He died some time between AD1 and AD200. He was sacrificed by being killed in three different ways, having been strangled, had his throat cut, and struck on the head. Like the three-mothers carving, this shows the Celts' use of the number three for religious purposes.

HORSES AND WAR

According to Roman writers, Epona was the Celtic goddess of war. Epona was worshipped by many Roman soldiers who spent time on duty in Celtic lands. This Roman-style carving shows Epona with a horse. It was found in northern France.

HUMAN SACRIFICE

Celtic priests, called druids, sometimes sacrificed human beings and animals as offerings to the gods. This scene from the Gundestrup bowl shows a giant-sized figure, maybe a god, holding a human sacrifice.

The famous Gundestrup bowl, which inspired your model, was made in eastern Europe some time between 200BC and 1BC. It was found many years later in a Danish bog.

THREE MOTHERS

To the Celts, the number three was a sign of power, so they often portrayed their gods and goddesses in triple form. This stone carving shows three mother-goddesses. It was made in Britain, probably between AD50 and AD400. The figures stand for the three female qualities of strength, power and fertility.

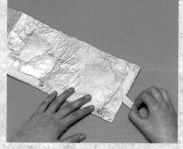

4 Cover both sides of the card strip and the plasticine figures with glue. Then cover with silver foil. Make sure that the foil is well glued to the figures.

5 Stick double-sided tape to the back of the foil-covered strip along the bottom and side edges. This will be used to join the sides of the bowl.

6 Make holes with a bradawl every few centimetres through the bottom of the strip. Make matching holes along the top of the bowl, as shown.

7 Attach the strip to the bowl with the double-sided tape. Stick the ends together, as shown. Secure by putting paper fasteners through both sets of holes.

The Celtic Year

AS FARMERS, the Celts needed to be able to measure time, so that they would know when to plough their fields and sow their crops. The Celtic year (354 days) was divided into 12 months, each 29 or 30 days long. Every two-and-a-half years, an extra month was added, so that the Celts' year kept pace with the natural seasons. The Celts also marked the passing of time by holding religious festivals. Samain (1 November) was the most important. It was the beginning of the Celtic year, and was a time for sacrifices and community gatherings. It was a dangerous time, when spirits walked the earth. Samain has survived today in Christian form as All Souls' Day, and Hallowe'en. Imbolc (1 February) marked the beginning of springtime and fertility. Beltane (1 May) was observed by lighting bonfires. Their smoke had purifying powers, and was used to kill pests on cattle. The final festival of the year was Lugnasad (1 August).

GODDESS AND SAINT
This statue is of the Celtic goddess Brigit (later known as St Brigit in Ireland) who was honoured at Imbolc. The Celts believed that she brought fertility and fresh growth. She was also the goddess of learning, and had healing powers.

HOLY DAYS
Celtic calendars were kept by druids (priests). They believed that some days were fortunate, while others brought bad luck. This picture, painted about 150 years ago, shows how one artist thought a druid might look. However, it is mostly imaginary.

MAKE A PIG

You will need: modelling clay, board, modelling tool, ruler, 4 x balsa-wood sticks, metallic paint, paintbrush.

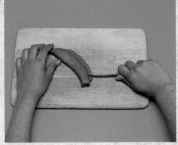

1 Make the body of the pig by rolling a piece of modelling clay into a sausage shape roughly 13 cm x 3.5 cm. Make a head shape at one end.

2 With your thumb and index finger, carefully flatten out a ridge along the back of the pig. The ridge should be about 1 cm high.

3 Now use the modelling tool to make a pattern along the ridge section. The pattern should have straight vertical lines on both sides of the ridge.

CLEVER GOD

Archaeologists think that this stone head, found in North Wales, may represent Lug, the Celtic god of all the arts. According to legend, Lug was clever at everything. He was honoured at Lugnasad, the fourth and final festival of the Celtic year when offerings were made to all the earth spirits and goddesses, to ask them for a plentiful harvest.

MISTLETOE AND OAK

Both mistletoe and oak were sacred to the Celts. Druids made sacrifices at wooden temples or in sacred oak groves. Even the druids' name meant "knowledge of the oak". Mistletoe was magic and mysterious. It could only be cut with a golden sickle. Mistletoe growing on oak trees was the most holy and powerful of all.

mistletoe   *oak tree leaves*

DRUID CEREMONY

This picture from the 1800s shows an imaginary view of druids at a Celtic religious ceremony. We have very little detailed information about how these ceremonies were performed. According to Roman writers, there were three different kinds of druids, each with different duties. Some were soothsayers, who told the future and issued warnings. Some held sacrifices. Some wrote and performed songs in honour of the gods.

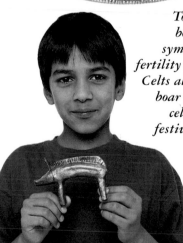

To the Celts, wild boars were magic symbols of strength, fertility and power. The Celts also enjoyed roast boar at feasts held to celebrate the great festivals of the Celtic year, such as Samain, Imbolc, Beltane and Lugnasad.

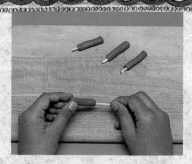

4 Roll out four legs roughly 4.5 cm long. Push a balsa-wood stick into each leg. Leave about 1 cm of balsa wood exposed, as shown.

5 Now roll out a small amount of modelling clay. Cut out two triangular shapes using your modelling tool. These will be the pig's ears.

6 Carefully attach the ears on either side of the pig's head. Mould them on using a little water and your modelling tool, as shown.

7 Attach the legs to the pig, pushing the balsa wood sticks into the body. Leave the modelling clay to dry. When it is dry, paint the whole pig.

The Magic Realm

THE CELTS BELIEVED IN life after death. When a man or woman died, the soul left the body and journeyed to a magic realm of ghosts and spirits. After a time of rest in the realm, the dead person's spirit might be reborn as a new baby or, possibly, as an animal or a bird. Beliefs varied from place to place, but many Celtic peoples thought that the period soon after someone's death was a dangerous time for their relatives and friends. The dead person's spirit was trapped close to their body, and might cause harm. However, after the dead person's flesh had finally rotted away, their spirit was set free, and could help and protect people close to them. Bones from long-dead ancestors were sometimes kept by their relatives like lucky charms.

From about 700BC to 100BC, the Celts of mainland Europe buried dead bodies in the earth. Usually, the body was carefully arranged on a bed of dried grasses and flowers, dressed in clean clothes, and surrounded by treasured possessions. In the British Isles, burial customs were different. Sometimes, bodies were laid on a wooden frame in the open air until the flesh rotted away from their bones (this is called excarnation). Then the bones were buried. Sometimes, whole bodies were placed, along with others, in disused stone buildings or caves. After around 100BC, customs changed and cremation became popular throughout the Celtic world.

FOR THE FUNERAL FEAST
When an important person died, it was the duty of their relatives to hold a funeral feast. Large quantities of wine or mead (honey wine) were served to the dead person's followers from huge kraters (mixing vessels). This krater was imported from Greece. It held 1,100 litres of wine and water.

BURIED WITH A PRINCE
Only a very rich person could afford gold and iron in Celtic times. This golden bowl and iron dagger in a gold-plated sheath were buried in the grave of a prince at Hochdorf, in Germany, in about 540BC. The dagger's blade is bent and twisted. This may have been to "kill" its power, so that it could rest in the grave with its owner. The prince's wife was also killed, and buried alongside her husband.

RITUAL PIT

From around 400BC, the Celts dug deep pits at holy sites, into which they threw the remains of human bodies, sacrificed animals and offerings of pottery, wood and metal. These were probably all gifts to the gods. Most ritual pits have been found in southern France, but they have been discovered in many other Celtic lands.

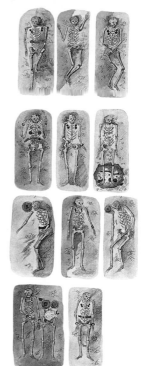

TOMB MOUND

During the Hallstatt era (750–450BC), many important Celts were buried under huge earth mounds, called barrows. Inside, there was a wood-lined burial chamber, surrounded by smaller spaces where family members could be buried later on. This picture shows an early prehistoric burial mound, based on the knowledge available to people in the 1800s and mixed with quite a lot of imagination. Today, archaeologists know that Hallstatt mounds did not have side entrances and were not surrounded by standing stones.

LAID TO REST

This modern reconstruction shows a burial in central France, around 700BC. The dead chieftain is wrapped in a woollen blanket. Loyal followers have placed his sword and a finely-made bucket of wood and bronze nearby. A rich display of grave goods at a burial demonstrated the dead chief's wealth.

CHANGING CUSTOMS

After cremation, the ashes of a dead person were collected up and placed in a pottery urn like this one. The pot containing the ashes was then buried in the ground. No one knows for sure why cremations replaced burials. The Celts may have come to believe that cremation made it easier for the soul to escape from the body. Or they may have been copying Roman burial customs.

Missionaries and Monks

IN MAINLAND EUROPE, Celtic power was destroyed by AD1. From that time, the former Celtic lands were ruled by Rome. After around AD400, the Roman Empire in turn was attacked by tribespeople from beyond its frontiers. Germanic peoples, such as the Angles, Saxons and Franks, took control of north-western Europe, while the Slavs controlled east European lands. Celtic languages and artistic traditions survived for up to 200 years after the Roman invasions but, by about AD400, they had almost disappeared. In the British Isles, the situation was different. Northern and western Scotland, and the whole of Ireland, were never conquered by Rome or invaded by Germanic tribes after Roman power collapsed. Celtic languages and traditions survived there, and mingled with a new faith, Christianity (brought to the British Isles during the time the Romans ruled), to create a final flowering of Celtic culture.

ALONE TO PRAY
Leaders of the Christian Church in Ireland and Scotland encouraged men and women to live in religious communities, apart from the rest of the world, where they could devote their lives to God. Many Celtic monks built little beehive-shaped cells out of rough stone, where they could spend time alone in peace and quiet. This cell is at Cloghan, in Ireland.

SCOTLAND'S TEACHER
Christianity first reached Ireland between AD400 and AD450, where it was spread by missionaries such as St Patrick. After St Patrick's death, Irish missionaries, including St Columba (shown here in a modern stained-glass window), carried Christian teachings to Scotland and other lands.

STRAP WORK
You will need: card 40 cm x 60 cm, ruler, pencil, felt-tip pen, paint and paintbrushes, rubber, water, water pot.

1 On the card draw a rectangle 57 cm x 37 cm. Draw lines 1 cm in from the long sides and 1.5 cm in from the short sides. Draw lines 9.5 cm in from each end.

2 Divide the border area you have created into two horizontally. At the far left and right ends draw lines 3.5cm in. Now draw three other lines at 7 cm intervals.

3 Begin in the top right-hand corner of the top section. Place your pencil at the intersection of the first four squares. Draw the design shown above.

IN CELTIC STYLE

The *Book of Kells* is a Christian text with Celtic decorations. It was made in about AD800, probably at the monastery on the Scottish island of Iona. The detail on some pages is so fine that it can hardly be seen by the naked eye. Books like these, written by Celtic monks in Old Irish and Latin, helped to preserve ancient Celtic words and ideas and it is thanks to these monks that so many Celtic traditions survived. As well as copying out many Christian texts, they also wrote down many ancient Celtic myths and legends, recording them for future generations to read.

ST MARTIN'S CROSS

Tall crosses were used to mark Christian burials, and as preaching places or border-posts on the edge of holy ground. Sometimes Celtic standing stones were turned into crosses. In other cases fresh stonework was carved. Like many other early crosses, St Martin's cross was decorated with Celtic patterns. It was made in about AD700 in Iona. There are slots cut into the ends of the crossways arms which may once have held decorative metal pieces.

BEAUTIFUL BOOK

The *Book of Durrow* is a Christian book decorated with Celtic designs. It was made in Iona in about AD675. Parts of it are said to have been written by St Columba.

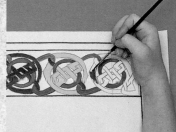

Copy a few Gaelic words on to your manuscript: "And pray for Mac Craith, King of Cashell". Interlaced designs such as this one are found in manuscripts decorated in the Celtic style.

4 Add two outer circles to your design, as shown. Join the circles to the open ends of your design to create an "endless knot".

5 Add two larger circles and the corner designs to your endless knot, as shown. Extend the open ends on the left of the design to begin a second knot.

6 Use the same method to create a row of knots. Use the grid as a guide. Next draw a row of knots in the section along the bottom of the card.

7 Paint the different strands of knot using typical Celtic colours such as green and red. When the border is completely dry, rub out the pencil grid.

Glossary

A

aerial From the air.

alloy A mixture of metals melted together to create a new substance.

amber The fossilized resin from pine trees. Amber was very highly prized by the Celts.

amphora A tall pottery jar used to store wine. Its plural is "amphorae".

archaeologist Someone who studies the past by looking at ancient objects and the physical remains, such as ruins, left by past civilizations.

B

barbarians Wild, rough and uncivilized people. The word was invented by the ancient Greeks to describe people who did not speak their language or follow their lifestyle. The Greeks thought that the spoken languages of these people sounded like "bar, bar".

bards In Celtic times, bards were well-educated poets. Becoming a bard was the first stage in the long training to be a druid.

boar A wild pig.

broch A tall, round stone tower built by the Celts in Scotland. Brochs were probably originally built as safe places for people to shelter in wartime.

bronze A metal alloy, made from a mixture of copper and tin.

C

carnyx A Celtic war trumpet.

cauldron A huge cooking pot.

causeway A raised walkway.

chainmail Small rings of metal, linked together to form a fine mesh, used to protect the body during battle.

citadel A stronghold.

clans Families who trace their descent from a single ancestor, and who share ties of loyalty and a family name.

cliff castle A Celtic fort and lookout post built on top of a cliff.

coracle A small boat made of leather stretched across a wooden frame.

crannog Small, artificial islands that the Celts built in lakes.

cremation The process of burning dead bodies.

D

dictator A sole ruler.

dismantled Taken to pieces.

dowry Money that is given to a newly-married couple, usually by the bride's father.

druids Celtic priests. According to Roman writers, there were three different grades of druid. Some studied the natural world and claimed to foretell the future. Some were bards who knew about history. Some led Celtic worship, made sacrifices to the gods, and administered holy laws.

F

firedogs Ornamental metal props used to hold logs in place on an open fire.

G

grid A rectangular pattern made by straight lines crossing each other at right angles.

H

Hallstatt era The early part of the Celtic period, dated from around 750 to 450BC. It is named after a place in Austria.

harness The leather straps that are used to attach horses to chariots or other vehicles.

hilt The handle of a sword.

hoe A sharp blade fitted to a long pole. It is used to kill weeds that are growing amongst crop plants.

I

imported Brought from abroad.

induce To bring something about.

iron ore The rock that contains iron in a raw, natural form. Before the iron can be used, the ore has to be crushed and then heated to release the metal.

iron-shod Something that is bound with iron.

K

krater A large ancient Greek bowl used for mixing wine and water together.

L

La Tène era The late part of the Celtic period, dated from around 450 to 50BC.

latticed In a criss-cross pattern.

lyre An ancient musical instrument that is played by plucking its strings.

M

marl Natural lime, dug from under the ground.

mead An alcoholic drink made from honey.

missionary Someone who tries to convert others to their own religious beliefs.

molten Something that is melted.

O

Ogham The Celtic writing system, based on the Latin alphabet.

oppida The Roman name for Celtic towns.

P

parasite In Celtic times, the low-ranking follower of a chieftain. His duty was to praise the chieftain, especially before a battle.

pedestal A stand that supports an object.

Picts A mysterious people who lived in Scotland from about AD300 to AD900. They were descended from earlier Celts.

plunder Stolen goods.

prow The front end of a boat.

Q

quern A simple machine, made from two stones, that is used to grind corn.

R

ramparts Steep earth banks.

relics Items associated with famous or holy people.

reliquary A container for holy objects such as relics.

repoussé A metalworking technique that is used to create decorative raised patterns on a metal object.

reputedly According to legend or unconfirmed reports.

S

scabbard The container for a sword-blade. It is usually fixed to a belt.

severed Cut off.

shield boss The metal plate that is fixed to the centre of a shield in order to protect the hand of the person holding the shield.

shift A plain, straight and very simple dress.

shrine A holy place where gods are worshipped.

sickle A large, sharp curved knife.

slats Strips of wood.

soldered Something that is joined together with small pieces of melted metal.

spatula A blunt knife used for scooping and spreading.

standard-bearer A soldier who carries an army's flag or emblem (special badge) into battle.

status symbols Signs of wealth and power.

sumptuous Rich and splendid.

T

talisman A lucky charm.

terret ring A ring that is fixed to a chariot, through which reins pass.

torc A heavy necklace. The Celts believed that torcs had magic, protective powers.

trance The state of being asleep yet conscious.

tribe A group of families who owe loyalty to a chief.

triumphal arch A large archway, built to honour a conquering army and its commander on their return from war.

V

vallus The Roman name for a Celtic farm machine, used for reaping (cutting) grain crops.

W

wattle and daub A building material made from woven twigs and branches covered with a paste made of clay, mud and sometimes animal dung.

woad A blue dye, made from plants, used by the Celts to paint or tattoo their skin.

Index